Counselling Young People

Counselling Young People

ELLEN NOONAN

Methuen
London and New York

First published in 1983 by
Methuen & Co. Ltd
11 New Fetter Lane, London EC4P 4EE
Published in the USA by
Methuen & Co.
in association with Methuen, Inc.
733 Third Avenue, New York, NY 10017
© 1983 Ellen Noonan
Printed in Great Britain by
Richard Clay & Co. Ltd,
Bungay, Suffolk

British Library Cataloguing in Publication Data

Noonan, Ellen
  Counselling young people.
  1. Social work with youth - Great Britain
  2. Counselling - Great Britain
  I. Title
  362.7   HV1441.G7

ISBN 0-416-36210-9
ISBN 0-416-36220-6 Pbk

Contents

I sat down to turn out a small cupboard and found it was like Pandora's Box – and there I was, flinging away misguided notions, misconceptions, useless expectations. When I came back home again I looked at my room, and it was full of rubbish. What was I keeping all this for? I threw all that stuff out . . . I've experimented at everything this term, done everything I wanted to do, not always well, but I've done it and I'm glad. But I look around and see others scaling the top of the mountain, and I'm wandering aimlessly around and around the bottom slopes. And I have an awful sense of regret – that years from now I'll look back and think I missed this opportunity and chose to do the wrong thing. I'm nearly twenty-one and I'm at Oxford. What I thought was the end of the road is just fleeting. Three years is only one more than two years. I'm where social movements matter. It used to be that they only happened to other people, like accidents, but now they affect me – the role of women, that sort of thing. But what if I fling away the wrong thing – I would be betraying myself. How do I know what to keep? Maybe the very things I'm losing, giving up, will be the things I'll really want later.

MANDY
*on her adolescence and
her counselling*

Preface and acknowledgements

Counselling has its beginnings, both historically as an emerging discipline and daily as a particular activity, in many different professions. It fills the space between psychotherapy and friendship, and it has become a recognized extension of the work of almost everyone whose business touches upon the personal, social, occupational, medical, educational and spiritual aspects of people. Because, like Topsy, it just grew, because it falls as much within the province of bringing on the already well-functioning as that of diminishing distress, and because it refers to people who are counsellors and others who apply counselling skills as they deem appropriate, there is no unified concept of its work. Indeed, the literature on counselling is a rather motley and intriguing array. This seems to be a good and stimulating state of affairs, but it is also frustrating for anyone wanting to find everything about counselling between two covers. This addition to the literature arises partly because I, as a trainer, wanted an introductory text which would cover all the territory essential to counsellors. As such, of course, this book only compounds the diversity of approaches since what I regard as essential is particular to my experience, theoretical predilection and interests. Others in search of the perfect book for their requirements may have to go on looking, but they are invited to read this if they are interested in the theory and practice of psychoanalytically based counselling of young people. The ideas contained here have so far been useful to many students, on many courses – and in a quite different way to our clients – but usefulness depends to some extent on the credibility of the speaker, the readiness of the listener to share the framework, and the match between what is needed and what is offered, so it is only fair to set out here the general intentions of the book.

This is not a textbook, although it has a comprehensiveness in including the three broad areas of critical concern to counsellors: theory, practice and professional matters. It begins by considering the process of change, since this is an inescapable feature of the lives of young people, and, if all goes well, of counselling. Next comes an exposition of the central themes of psychoanalytic theory, drawing mainly from the work of Klein and Winnicott who seem to have the most accessible models for personal and interpersonal relationships, especially for understanding the preoccupations of young people. In the middle part of the book, the focus is on what happens between client and counsellor at work: the kinds of relationship they establish, their ways of communicating with each other, and how the work can lead to change. The third part concentrates on the counsellor as a professional person who has standards to meet, personal needs to manage, and a work setting which impinges on her work with clients and colleagues. The organization of the book itself reflects my opinion that we need theory first as a framework for making sense of what our clients say and do, and for providing sound strategies for what we do. Client work is unquestionably central and demands the best of our working energy and creativity, but it is not - and cannot be - practised in a vacuum, so the counsellor needs to be well in touch with her professional and organizational reality.

The sort of counselling discussed here is work with individuals carried out within a formal structure, ranging from very brief contacts to intensive engagements lasting over several years. The ideas and illustrations are accumulated from my experience in hospitals, clinics, guidance units, industry, professional trainings and universities. Although the balance is weighted toward work with people who seek help in a state of distress or conflict, the principles and procedures are equally applicable to work in less formal settings, and with people who are evidently successful in life and wish to enhance their effectiveness. The counselling presented works for the whole spectrum because it is that variety of verbal therapy where the client explores his life and feelings, and the counsellor offers an understanding of the personal meaning of his experience, conscious or unconscious. Both are attempting to comprehend his internal world in relation to his past, present and future, and the aim is change, a new perspective, and the gaining of insight and emotional freedom which can lead to real changes in relating and behaving.

Much of the content may seem to be about psychotherapy rather than counselling. That may be so. This is a blurred territorial boundary and in practice it cannot be drawn according to rigid abstract arguments. Criteria such as goals, techniques, the quality of involvement and depth of exploration are invoked in discussion to distinguish the two, most usually to support the position that psychotherapy is deeper, more ambitious, and technically more demanding than counselling. The motive for these deliberations seems to be the twin-headed monster of professional rivalry and anxiety about the damage which can ensue from meddling in the lives and feelings of the vulnerable. No 'vulnerable' person, whether called a client or a patient, will respect arbitrary boundaries, and he is surely more concerned with competence than with titles – as we ought to be. Nearly everyone who comes to see us brings a reality problem to be sorted out and an unconscious to be explored, an anxiety to be relieved and a phantasy to be untangled, an acute need to be helped and a transference relationship to be tested out. What we do, what level we work at, what technique we bring, what outcome we envisage depend on where the client's urgency and transparency lie, what depth he can tolerate at the moment, and what kind of relationship we can establish. All these can vary from moment to moment, or month to month; titles are superfluous. The only criteria which make sense are those linked to responsibility. Whatever levels, techniques or goals are chosen, they cannot be chosen capriciously, but must have good intuitive *and* theoretical intentions which can be articulated. Anyone who works with the increasingly subjective material of phantasy, the inner world and the unconscious must first have explored his or her own unconscious therapeutically in order that understanding of the other's material is not cluttered and distorted by the unknown preoccupations of the self. It is impossible to be over-trained or over-'therapied' in this work. Consequently this book may appeal equally to counsellors and psychotherapists, and to those who consider counselling as only one part of their work. Additionally, because so many young people who seek help are students, and because many of the themes are illustrated with examples from the university setting, it may be particularly relevant to those working in educational institutions.

I have said that this is not a textbook: it is not detailed and orderly enough to qualify for that designation. Each chapter could be a volume in its own right, so I tend to think of it as a series of elliptical passages – a record of some fascinating ideas which have stood the test of time in serving clients and counsellors well. Some areas have been treated in a fairly simple introductory manner; some have been pursued at greater depth; and some, which others might consider absolutely essential, have been taken for granted or omitted in favour of themes which seem significant to me.

Many trainees in this field have had sobering moments of discovering that the gap between thinking they knew what their mentors were talking about and putting it into practice was dismally large. I recall a very disconcerting phase with a new supervisor, whom I knew to be wise, when I imagined him sitting behind me in my sessions, and wincing as I mangled his understanding of my clients. Not until I could translate his concepts into my own language and his techniques into my personal style did he cease to intrude and become useful to me. The moral of this anecdote is an acknowledgement that we have essentially personal relationship with our theory and practice. It is self-evident that anything so intensely engaging as counselling has to rely on an immediate and very human commitment. Therapeutic schools are primarily identified with the names of the people who developed the ideas, and the acrimony which has sometimes accompanied the diversification and elaboration of theory bears witness to the fact that there is a strong personal element underlying the empirical observations and intellectual discipline. This does not necessarily diminish the value of the theories, although the limited amount of systematic research in this area leaves us accepting or rejecting them on the basis of whether or not they work in practice. Most of us do not enjoy the creativity of the founders of therapeutic schools, but it is still open to us to have the gratification of having a living relationship with our work: we can expand and modify received wisdom as a result of our experience and in response to the demands of our work. We will inevitably focus on aspects which are personally significant, and we will respond to an approach which makes best sense of our life-events and best fits our personal style. But this kind of work is not a narcissistic enterprise, and I would be deeply suspicious of anyone who failed to expose his work to the scrutiny of colleagues. Similarly, I would mistrust anyone who attempted to use any book such as this to circumvent his own individual struggle with the ideas and feelings aroused by the daily encounter with individuals in distress; it can only be a catalyst in that struggle.

I am acutely aware of my debt to all those, both in person and in books, who have taught me. As I was writing I found I could not disentangle what came from where or from whom, except the clients who stand out as very distinct individuals, some of them teaching me very specific things, and they have been camouflaged. My solution has been to attribute very little in the text, but to list in the bibliography sources which have made an impact on my work or which pursue ideas only touched upon. My actual professional grandparents, parents, siblings and children have been mainly in the Adult Department of the Tavistock Clinic and in the University of London Student Counselling Course, and it would be right for them to feel that they have a tangible and much appreciated share in this book; if any recognize themselves, I hope the work represented here stands as an act of true gratitude. I do want, however, to single out Sadie Gillespie and David Malan as two people who most generously placed their skills and sensitivity at my disposal as I was, and am, learning. And, as I wrote, it was Brenda Lewis who encouraged me to go on when it seemed a silly thing to do, and Victor Hood who gently handed me down from personal and professional hobby-horses. My secretary, Maureen Gilbert, deciphered the drafts with tact and good humour; and friends kindly lent me their cottage in the country, where I could find distance and peace to write and refresh myself simultaneously.

Throughout I have referred to the counsellor as 'she' and the client as 'he' for the sake of clarity in general discussion. Needless to say, the sexes do not always distribute themselves so, but I am a 'she' and it was just easier to write that way.

1 | Adolescent to adult: the transition period

We are accustomed to think about adolescents as storming and stressing, rebelling, being difficult or the hope of the future, indiscriminately consuming the latest fad, causing anxiety by unpredictable or incomprehensible behaviour, or being over-sensitive and morose or callous and boisterous in their relationships. While understanding that they are 'going through a crisis' which they will no doubt 'out-grow', we still feel impatient and irritated with the awkwardness they create around them, and with their apparent refusal to settle down to a 'reasonable', even-keeled existence. The myth that this is the best time of life – generated in large part by wistful envy from elders tarnished by life, or by youngsters still unschooled in life – dies hard, and we can't quite understand why they aren't a happier lot of young people, excited by their current privilege and anticipating what lies ahead. Indeed, we rather think adolescents should celebrate their state as we traditionally celebrate New Year: a noisy night of elation proceeding with clockwork certainty to the midnight hour. At this time we look for omens of the future in our horoscopes or in local customs, hoping that next year will be better, or at least not worse than this year. Incited by the magic-borne possibilities, and knowing that we needn't work tomorrow, we give ourselves up to irresponsible carousing, and for a brief moment we put our arms around each other to sing 'Auld Lang Syne' as if it were a time of well-being and *bonhomie*.

While some of us are out celebrating, however, others of us are sitting at home feeling depressed and uncomfortably out of line with the 'normal' celebrants. We are suffering regret for what has truly gone, for ambitions unfulfilled, for errors unamended, for what might have been, and we are apprehensive about our ability to manage life any differently next year. Slim consolation comes from the recollection of achievements and pleasures and from the sense of having learned something from our experience.

It is right that we should mark the New Year, of course, and it is perhaps no accident that we have such an exuberant ritual to help us through this night of uncertainty, to help us put out of our mind two very uncomfortable facts of life: our romantic, domestic, work and our financial future are not determined by magic but by our own resources for making what we can of the world we live in; and the year gone by is lost for ever and can never be replaced. 'Auld Lang Syne' is a song of mourning, so we may well hold on to what is present and sing it boisterously in order not to know that, with the striking of the clock, we have just lost something and are faced with a future which we cannot predict with any certainty.

The sense of hopefulness and sadness exists in all of us, of course, although each of us may tip the balance in his own particular way, experiencing one more than the other. Similarly, the young person in that maturational space between childhood and adulthood cannot divide himself, but must hold within himself both the regretful and anticipatory aspects of transition. Adolescence is a period of transition, and it is characterized by acute feelings of anxiety and uncertainty alongside excitement. Habitual ways of relating to others and accustomed ideas about the self and the world are becoming outdated and must be relinquished, but no sure substitutes are readily to hand. Attempts to hold on to old patterns result in disconcerting and frustrating experiences because the world is changing and a conservative stance puts the individual out of step. It is equally impossible to be single-mindedly excited by the future – the material gains of learning and earning, sexual possibilities, legal privileges, and autonomous strength – because the adolescent does not yet know how he will use these things nor how he will be used by them. Such anxiety and uncertainty promote precipitate actions, withdrawal, anger, inconsistency, depression and euphoria.

Because of these mood-swings and the force behind them, it may be as discomforting to be in the presence of an adolescent as it is to be with someone who is grief-stricken – it is, in this society, neither sightly nor seemly to mourn publicly. Even the thought of personal mourning tends to make most people feel uncomfortable and helpless, so mourning has been forced underground. (In recognition of the work of people like Colin Parkes (1972), however, it should be said that death now begins to exert a fascination, and we are becoming more able to tolerate feelings about the reality of death.) Similarly, adolescence is often considered a subversive, underground activity, usually viewed obliquely, its real substance concealed and revealed only by surface manifestations which sometimes appear unsightly and unseemly, both literally and metaphorically. The resemblance between grief and adolescence is more than superficial, however, since the adolescent transition is as much about loss as it is about gain.

MOURNING: A MODEL FOR TRANSITION

The active and emotionally energetic process of mourning provides a model for the adolescent transition, since both are attempts to achieve a sense of personal continuity out of the confusion of drastic disruption. By extension, of course, it also becomes a model for therapeutic change. It is easiest to see and describe the mourning process when the loss is stark, when someone actually dies and cannot be retrieved in any physical way. The survivor is faced with a dilemma: of letting the dead person go while still giving him space in life as a living if not palpable being; of accepting the discontinuity in life while striving to maintain continuity into the future. Keeping himself firmly in the present, the mourner has to look backwards and forward simultaneously.

In the ordinary and healthy process of mourning, the griever withdraws, seeking time and space to concentrate on his loss and on the lost person. This is a time of intense struggle with the conflicting claims of the past and future, conflicts which are resolved by consolidating what is meaningful and significant from the past and finding some meaning for the future in this new depleted state. Personal history is reviewed, events and feelings once shared with the deceased are revived and relived. This is a bitter-sweet experience because there is now no chance of repeating those pleasures and no opportunity to make good the flaws and failures. It is tempting, then, to jettison the past and look to the possibilities of the future, but the very thought of this brings guilt-laden feelings of betrayal and desertion toward the absent one, so the griever is dragged back to contemplation of the past. The dead person is recalled with all the feelings felt before, he may even be perceived as actually present, definitely here and separate, still a partner in the business of sorting out the problems of living; but this illusion offers only a temporary respite from the reality of death.

During this emotional involvement with the past, however, time goes on inexorably. Although apparently meaningless without the lost person and the lost relationship, life has to go on, decisions need to be made, relationships have to be continued, albeit in an altered form. Awareness of the real emptiness in the past helps the survivor to face the anxieties and uncertainties of the present and future. At the time of a death, the threat comes as much from feeling that part of the self has been lost as from the actual loss of the other person. It is no mere cliché to say 'I feel as if part of myself has gone' because we do invest parts of ourselves in others, and we do define ourselves to some extent by the relationships we have.

In a traditional marriage, for instance, the husband may take on the responsibility for dealing with the external world of taxes, bills and arranging for services, and therefore expresses the aggressive and demanding feelings for the couple, while the wife has responsibility for care and comfort within the house, expressing the nurturing feelings. The more intimately involved the two are, and the more mutually exclusive the 'division of labour' of roles and feelings is, the more the survivor is likely to feel that part of himself disappeared with the death of the partner and to feel anxious about doing and being what the partner has up until now expressed on his behalf. The feeling of helplessness which often accompanies a bereavement arises partly from this sense of no longer being able to function in an established identity and having to extend the self to include those 'delegated' aspects which are certainly out of practice and probably were not wanted anyway.

Gradually the survivor finds within himself some attributes and attitudes of the dead person and no longer needs to relive and maintain the past in concrete ways because that person is 'alive' inside as a set of memories, ideas and feelings. As this happens, it becomes possible to let go of the physical images and the compulsion to fidelity. This internalization alleviates anxieties about betrayal and reorganizes internal patterns; new meanings and attachments develop in the new context. A revised identity and an altered view of the world preserves the thread of meaning.

In mourning, flight into activity directed toward the future and retreat into broodiness about the past are neither, in themselves, satisfactory, but the to-ing and fro-ing in response to relentless nudges in both directions – and the attendant feelings of sadness, anger, guilt, happiness, love and hope – is the process though which loss is acknowledged and conflict is reconciled. Death or loss is a major environmental event which severely disrupts the flow of life, and continuity has to be restored by this internal activity in the survivor. By incorporating this experience and the feelings about it in himself, the survivor ensures a continuing sense of himself in the world; he accommodates an experience which originally seemed to threaten his very existence; he manages to make sense of something 'senseless'; he finds new meaning for the future through the phase of disorientation; through loss he is enriched.

LOSS AND GAIN IN ADOLESCENCE

It may seem that adolescence is a long way from this; from an irreversible loss which occurs at a defined point in time; from an endeavour to tolerate the conflict of the pulls of the past and future while remaining still in the present. However, we can sometimes feel that our childhood has been irretrievably lost. For instance we can return to our family, home and childhood haunts and relationships, but they will never be as they were when we left them, because we and they have done things in the meantime. The meeting is between changed, different people, and it is often disappointing, almost as if the past has betrayed us by altering. It is tempting to want to put the clock back and to reinstate the old order, but that can only ever be partially successful because it is impossible to shed the effects of time and experience. Instead we tend to adapt to the disconcertingly unfamiliar familiarity, and we can do this because we have a sense of 'this is me' which has enabled us to assimilate a variety of experiences, accepting the change they make in us without losing touch with the old order. The return, then, becomes another new experience, not a reversion.

Personal maturation requires some things to be yielded to make way for new ones; it requires us to convert childhood into a memory which is alive, if not palpable, inside us, and this means we have to mourn aspects of our child-self so they may be internalized. Change and gain involve the same ambivalent process as loss does: space needs to be made for new experience, just as the gap created by loss needs to be bridged. In both, continuity is established by looking back longingly to how it was, and looking ahead uncertainly to life as it will be, and continually reinterpreting ourselves and the world in the light of new developments. Not to do so, not to spend time and energy on weaving this individual thread of meaning, leaves us in a falsely based, defensive existence, where the whole aim becomes simply to survive change.

For the adolescent loss and gain are cumulative and progressive. The changes vary from the acute to the creeping, from the insistent to the whispering. Each individual will have his own idiosyncratic pace and attach his own meanings to what happens; but, generally speaking, we can look at the varieties of change ordinarily experienced by everyone during this time.

SEXUALITY

New body shapes and physiological processes develop and have to be assimilated. This can be both exciting and disconcerting to the child, especially for those who have not been told, or have failed to 'hear', any information preparing them for the onset of puberty.

> Kate (despite being warned) managed to remain blissfully unaware of sexuality until she was awakened one morning by her first period. She was afraid to get up because her interpretation of the event was that all her insides had come loose and would tumble out if she stood up, rather like the stuffing coming out of her teddy bear when its seams had burst.

Others are better prepared, but even so a girl may naturally be preoccupied with the unpredictability of her periods until they settle into a pattern and she learns to make sense of the signs, both physical and emotional, sent out from her body. Over time, the information gained from parents and peers and her phantasies about her body-processes are matched against her own experience, and the change can be accepted and individualized, so she knows about, and can make reasonable predictions about, her body. The necessary extra care and attention to her body, if not to the calendar, which she was free from as a pre-pubertal child, are gradually accommodated into a daily pattern. When all goes well, her self-image is extended to include developing sexuality, and she delights in dreams of love, marriage and children.

Girls who have a shaky or ambivalent sense of themselves as feminine may be mostly angry and despairing about the loss of childhood asexuality and are quite unable to anticipate boyfriends, sexual relationships or motherhood with any pleasure.

> Julia, at twenty-one, wanted to be a cloud with eyes. Still feeling – and preferring to remain – an asexual child, she could find nothing positive in being female, much less sexual. She used contraceptive pills to manipulate and eliminate her periods, which were none the less experienced by her as an external enemy to be vanquished. So long as she refused them as a natural part of her growing and changing self, they were painful, disruptive episodes and the attentions of men (which were frequent and persistent because she was very pretty) felt irritating and senseless.

The onset of puberty perhaps takes boys less by suprise because male genital development is more visible. However, the recognition of sexual maturity may still be abrupt, as it was for Ted. He had been swimming with a group of boys during a holiday at the seaside. At the end of the day he was dragging his feet back to the shower, when suddenly he was aware that he *smelled* different: he smelled like a man. Horrified and confused, he dropped away from his friends and spent the rest of the holiday in a depressed and anxious state.

Changing body shapes publicly announce the arrival of sexuality, causing young people to be concerned with how they look both to themselves and to others. Hours of private contemplation of their body, and the ambivalent search for signs of change in it, are evidence of the healthy mourning process: they need to explore the newness, to regret differences between then and now, to adjust their self-image to accord with the physical change, and to indulge in the anxious excitement which accompanies the realization of sexual potential. Girls' attempts to make their breasts bigger than they are and then flatten them into non-existence, and boys' attempts to exhibit and hide erections are both very concrete ways of catapulting between the past and future in order to find sameness, to establish continuity, to identify 'me' between the two phases. Adolescents also become acutely aware of dress, and expend huge amounts of time and money on selecting garments that will reveal or conceal precisely the amount of sexuality they can psychologically accept at that moment. Running parallel to this are day-dreams and phantasies, built around facts, folklore, speculation, hopes and fears about the possibilities of life now that sexuality is a reality.

The private reconnaissance – including masturbation – is both a self-familiarization process and a rehearsal for real encounters with others. It is important to know our own body before someone else knows it, just as we want to explore and possess a gift before letting someone else handle it. If our awareness is pre-empted, initiative is lost and the result can feel like theft and spoilage: rather than coming from within and belonging to us, our responses and feelings seem to be mere reactions provoked by someone else.

> Julia consented to have 'art photos' taken of her by a photographer of short acquaintance. When she saw herself – psychologically for the first time – in the pictures, she felt enraged and bereft. He had appreciated her body before she had, and now it was, so to speak, a second-hand body to her, used and returned by him. Unable to use her sexual curiosity directly, she had disguised and yielded it to him, ultimately feeling exploited and deprived.

RELATIONSHIPS

Obviously rehearsal alone has limited usefulness: it can never take into account how others will actually behave and affect our thoughts and feelings about ourselves. Indeed, too much rehearsal leading to fixed and partial images can bring as much perplexity as too little awareness does, when it comes to the real thing. Friendships, therefore, become crucial testing grounds for developing self-images and private phantasies. Girls and boys talk with and question others of their own sex to assess and reflect their own sexual and personal development, and they grow increasingly curious about the other sex, wanting and needing to know just what sexuality is and how it will change relationships. Together they experiment with actions and feelings, shuttling between awful embarrassment and flagrant display. The intense single-sex relationships which characterize early adolescence are necessary to solidify a tenuous identity, but, if prolonged, they may be being used to deny change through an avoidance of the other sex, an inescapable reminder of difference and change and its consequences. Similarly sexual experimentation furthers the quest for knowledge, but, if premature, it becomes a denial of the uncertainty properly belonging to this phase of change and loss. The gradual and uneven progress from asexual childhood through same-sex groups, heterosexual groups, and into pairs, is the process through which the new physical, psychological and social realities gain acceptance and are comfortably integrated in their self-images. Information from within and without concurs, and they know where and who they are.

Increasing degrees of intimacy and commitment accompany the changes and evoke anxieties about betrayal as one group or individual is deserted for the next. The uncomfortable feelings of rejection, envy and jealousy – whether on the giving or receiving end – now seem more difficult to manage because they occur in the powerful, but vulnerable, area of sexuality among peers. The long-term future goals of marriage and parenthood, so long as these are attractive, help young people through the ups and downs, and enable them to make sense of buffeting experiences. Even so, there are times when it doesn't feel worth all the pain and anxiety, and retreat follows. But perpetual clinging to childhood does not permit their hopes to become realities, so they yield and re-enter the struggle. Those who do not have an attractive image of adulthood, like Julia, have little emotional incentive to stay with the struggle and can feel persecuted by the inexorable physiological process and social expectations.

Along with changes in relationships with peers, there are changes in the adolescent's relationships with parents and adults: changes in their interactions, in their attitudes toward themselves and each other, and in the internalized images of 'child' and 'adult'. In the ordinary family relationship, during the long phase of dependence, it is generally accepted that the child receives from providing parents. Parents make decisions for their child, doing what their experience and aspirations tell them is 'right'. This arrangement is not seriously questioned, but gradually the parents relinquish this role, and the child takes on more responsibility for self-provision and decision-making. Conflict – both within each person and between parents and child – inevitably occurs during the handing-over period because each will want to accomplish it at different rates, and the rates will vary from moment to moment and subject to subject, depending on the degree of safety and attractiveness involved.

Barbara was very keen to take responsibility for making appointments with the hairdresser, but not with the dentist. Equally, her parents were happy to let her decide how she spent her free time, but retained the right to dictate when she should study. She was a 'late developer', and her parents were pleased when she did arrange her own activities. They were horrified, however, when she fell madly in love and proposed to live with her first boyfriend. Family arguments resulted in mother and daughter not speaking, father trying to reason with her, and daughter virtually absenting herself by leaving early and returning late each day. She was utterly confused by their radically changed behaviour, and they were disappointed at this result of their liberal outlook. It all became explicable when it was revealed that the parents' relationship had begun in much the same way; they had given up education to support themselves, and their lives turned sterile very quickly. Mother's anger arose from a feeling of helplessness, and father was attempting to protect his daughter from making their mistake. Neither regarded their daughter as 'adult' enough to know the sad history of their marriage, so she was left confused.

Parent-child conflict is inevitable and necessary if the transfer of personal responsibility is to be genuine and enduring, if true autonomy is to be achieved. Adolescent rebellion (which carries negative overtones because the conflict *is* a threat to old established order) is the means by which the young person tests out values, attitudes, feelings and actions and so discovers how *he* feels, thinks and will be. The paradox, perhaps, is that this conflict which aims to dissolve the dominance of the parent-child tie has to begin firmly within the security of that relationship: it determines the boundary within which the struggle goes on and is as necessary as the ropes around a boxing ring. Both parties have to be willing to fight. In challenging parental values, the adolescent is asserting that he has to find his own values, but because he cannot completely dismiss those he grew up with he relies on the parents to embody and restate them. The ensuing disagreements and discussions are an external enactment of the adolescent's internal struggle.

Mathew grew increasingly bored and uncomfortable at school; he wasn't interested in the work and he felt 'different' from the others, even though he clearly liked some subjects and had much in common with his mates. He came from a well-educated family and he was bright so there was no question but that he would go to university. However, he was heading for failure at 'A' levels and he dedicated his intelligence to clever and bitter contempt for the shortcomings of his parents and their contemporaries, while secretly making enquiries about Oxbridge. He didn't quite fail exams, but was very distressed about his poor results because they ruined his chances for a good university. His parents were disappointed and disparaging. Mathew wanted there to be a question about his future; if everyone took it for granted, he felt he would never be seen as separate and different; if he did go on as expected he felt he was simply capitulating to their values, not doing it because he wanted to. In fact, Mathew did want what his parents wanted in the end, but in his efforts to spite his parents and to assert his individuality, he 'forgot' that he also valued academic achievement.

If the parents refuse to contend, or yield out of anxiety, the result for the child is catastrophic. In the first instance, he is deprived of the secure opposition for working out his concerns, and is left feeling abandoned by uncaring parents to the perils of an unknown and uncertain world. In the second, giving a child absolute freedom is no gift at all because it requires him to be eternally grateful to parents whose strength is untested and untrustworthy. The world 'out there' is unknown and uncertain, and the young person needs to be sure that when he sallies out into it and discovers new, startling or painful things, he can still return to a secure base to share and recover from his experience. In doing so, he discovers what his parents will share, tolerate or sympathize with, and he thus learns how he is both similar to and different from them. Through this process he finally separates himself from them and establishes his own dimensions. Similarly his internal world is unknown and uncertain, and he needs a secure base within which to discover the power and quality of his feelings. If he doesn't challenge he loses these opportunities, and he deprives his parents of their chance to modify and change as well.

This conflict with parents is sometimes fraught with anxieties about betrayal and seeming ingratitude.

Jane, in her first year at university, alarmed her tutor by simply coming to sit in her office, silent but refusing to leave. Invitations from other students to join their social activities increased these silent vigils, and Jane would only say she wanted to leave and return home, but her parents insisted she stay. When she could finally speak of her situation, it was complex and ironic. Jane was the only daughter of successful, small-village parents who, resenting their own lack of education, extolled the value of self-made success while making martyrish sacrifices for her to have private schooling. Her mother offered premature warnings about the dangers of drink, sex and wild urban life, while also deciding that she should study in London. Jane came up, was attracted by all the enticements of the city, and became terrified and confused. If she pursued all the possibilities before her, she would betray her parents by becoming all those things they rejected; if she turned away she would be wasteful and ungrateful for those years of sacrifice. She clung to her tutor in a desperate attempt to find some parental control for her 'evil' wishes, and she felt the only resolution was to return home to study locally, where she could avoid the conflict around whose terms would determine how she lived her life. It goes without saying that her parents were equally confused about what they wanted for her and for themselves, and the three had reached an impasse. Sadly Jane went home for the holidays and seriously damaged herself in an 'accident' which effectively stopped time. She hoped convalescence would be a suspended time when she could sort out herself and her relationship with her parents.

The conflict ultimately resolves itself by a process of negotiation. As each side asserts its views, it has to do so in a way the other will understand. *Rapprochement* occurs, if the relationship is to survive at all, simply through the need to communicate. Understanding, and perhaps identifying with, the other's view causes the nature of the relationship to change, and the challenge gives way to two adults - a new one and a 'reformed' one - talking to each other on the same level. The negotiation analogy perhaps implies that the process is diplomatic and polite, and rebellion seldom appears to be that. When both parents and child have the confidence to hold differing views and to argue about them, this is a position of mutual respect, regardless of its sometimes taking the form of an entrenched and bloody-minded battle to the death. Metaphorical death is indeed the aim, in the sense that the child-parent relationship is being removed from the present and taking its proper place in memory.

RESPONSIBILITY AND AUTHORITY

For the quality of the relationship to change, it is necessary for the images of adult and child to alter. This is most clearly demonstrated in the sphere of authority. The child is accustomed to attributing authority to the adult and believing in the validity of that authority. The adolescent questions that authority, often perceiving it as restrictive, anachronistic and wrong. As conflict develops, adults become the 'Them' of a 'Them and Us' pair. 'Them' is bad, reprehensible, hated; 'Us' is powerless, controlled, not responsible. When the adolescent arrives at the point of holding authority himself and having responsibility for decisions – of effectively becoming one of 'Them' – he must either change his view of 'Them', or take into himself those previously held negative attributes of 'Them' and become himself bad and hated. All his previous assumptions are invalidated or untenable; losing irresponsibility and being no longer able to regard power as beyond control gives rise to confusions and contradictions because the consequences of holding authority are personally unknown and the rewards may appear doubtful compared with the losses.

Peter had been job hunting in a listless way, quite sure he wouldn't get work, so he was surprised and delighted when he was offered one he wanted. He bought a new suit and set off in sober high spirits, but within a week he was depressed and anxious. The work wasn't as demanding as he had anticipated, yet he imagined that somehow the employer was disappointed with him. He believed he'd got the job out of sheer luck or because he had conned the employer as a result of practising interviewing with a careers advisor. The theme of deceit was familiar: as a schoolboy he had signed his father's name to his poor school reports. When his father discovered this, he gave the boy a good beating and a lecture, after which he came at the top of his class through the rest of his education. Authority for Peter was either punitive or demanding, images which he couldn't accept for himself, so he side-stepped his own responsibility by resorting to explanations based on luck or the 'borrowed' competence of the careers advisor.

Further complications arise when the adolescent has to take responsibility on behalf of his peers as well and has to identify with two groups simultaneously. The school prefect or student union officer, for instance, has to identify with the establishment and its decision-making capacity in order to fulfil his function in the system; but being a student and a representative of the students, he also has to identify with those for whom the decisions are being made. In order to be effective, he has to revise his view of authority as reprehensible and of himself as power-less, and in so doing he risks being accused of (or actually) betraying his peers. Adults are in an analogous position: they don't know the conse-quences of giving authority to the young people and are therefore reluctant and ready to be critical, especially if they are also representing other adults. Each side defends itself against uncertainty and anxiety by adhering rigidly to its old beliefs: the young say the adults are conser-vative bullies; the adults say the young are unrealistic and greedy. Each is pulled painfully backwards and forwards by the wish to stay with the familiar and the wish to develop.

BECOMING ADULT

As much as the adolescent may wish to gain independence and auto-nomy, his willingness to give up fundamental aspects of his identity as 'child' and to modify long-standing behaviour patterns depends on the image of 'adult' he holds and the fate he imagines for the 'child'. The inherent threat and uncertainty of change can give rise to precipitate actions and apparently irrational stances.

Jonathan felt that he had never had fun as a child; he had always done precisely as his parents had wanted, and now he was a good student who behaved as if the distractions of sexual and social rela-tionships were beneath him. As he neared the end of his postgra-duate degree (paid for by his parents and following his supervisor's research) he was acutely aware of his lack of spontaneity and social experience. Through counselling, he discovered that he could make his own decisions and implement his own plans, but he felt threatened by the possibilities and depressed by his inability to pursue them. He responded by making arrangements for national service, where he imagined he could again do what he was told, and free time would be joyous because it would be like being released from prison into 'obligatory' sexual experience.

While some find ways of circumventing change as Jonathan did, others make determined leaps into independence as a premature resolution adopted simply in order to be finished and done with all the chopping and changing of the transition phase.

Philip was a first-year university student living away from home for the first time. He was intensely homesick for his parents, home and girlfriend. He hadn't been able to make a considered decision about his course and arbitrarily but significantly chose his father's field. The course itself disappointed him, but rather than think through a change, he abruptly decided to leave university, return home, take a job in the civil service, save up to buy a house, and get married. He simply wanted to get settled as a working married man so he didn't have to bear the conflicts any longer: 'I've had enough of being an adolescent,' he said.

While Philip could probably successfully exchange adolescence for adulthood in this way, whether he would be happy in these acquisitions depends on his completing a psychological process which is more complicated than going through interviews and ceremonies. His decision had to be precipitate because he was not convinced that being an adult was as attractive and satisfying as being a child; he insisted upon catapulting himself forward in an over-zealous attempt to avoid dealing with his apprehension by a retreat into overt childhood dependence. In wishing to escape the painful conflicts of the transition phase, he psychologically experienced himself as ruthlessly murdering his child-self. In a repetitive dream he would come upon a scene of violence - a mass of dead people lying in the road, among them a boy whose head had been severed from his body. He was told that he had perpetrated the violence, and he recognized the decapitated boy as himself. This dream terrified him, but the same murderous process occurring in his studying depressed and bewildered him. As a boy he had ingeniously invented mechanical devices for the home, but now this creativity seemed to have died, and he was obsessional in his work, unable to connect ideas, to be enthusiastic, to think about the implications and applications of what he read.

The task of adolescence is not to kill off the child in this self-mutilating manner. Rather it is to leave the child in the past as a memory, and at the same time to retain modified capabilities and qualities which were originally developed in childhood. Those qualities – imagination, curiosity, and the capacity to lose oneself in play – are essential to learning, sexuality and achievement as an adult. Modifying them to fit adult needs provides continuity during change, and firmly links the present with the past and future. At the end of the process, the self-image should be at least as (if not more) capacious as before the change, loss and gain occurred.

By looking at the prevailing images of 'child' and 'adult', the reasons for Philip's feelings and actions become clear: while childhood has to be relegated to the status of memory kept alive through 'childish' qualities in the adult, that adulthood, which has until now only been a future possibility, has to become a present reality. This potential adult is primarily represented by the parents, and if they present an acceptable enough model, the child works consciously towards being that sort of adult. At the unconscious level, parental values and standards are internalized from the very beginning. As children are exposed to other adults they gain a multiplicity of models – some of whom are revered as idols and imitated, others rejected and ridiculed – comparisons are made, and qualities are selected for the compilation of the psychologically ideal adult self. Philip had grown up in a home which was at once limiting and unrestricted. His parents were strongly identified with their provincial community ruled by the church and school, both of which championed hard work, strict morality and traditional family solidarity. Within this setting, however, Philip was given considerable freedom to play while his mother exhausted herself looking after home and family and his father worked long, conscientious hours. Philip admired them, never questioned their values, had little experience of significantly different adults, and was too absorbed in his study and solitary play to become involved with the usual teenage idols. The contrast between child and adult was extreme. For him it didn't seem like a transition process; it felt more like exchanging the desirable for the undesirable, something he was morally obliged to do. Hence the apparent necessity to murder the child to make way for the adult. Everything had conspired to deprive him of his adolescence.

It is obvious that Philip's plans for the future were based on a spurious sense of autonomy. In genuinely evolved maturation the revised images and relationships subsume the old ones. The dual possibilities within dependence and independence, relatedness and autonomy, and authority and reliance exist simultaneously, each readily available as circumstances require. Although the actual parents have been put aside, they have not been rejected entirely; the parental model is retained in memory along with the child.

Perhaps the analogy of rearranged furniture in a familiar room is a more fitting one for adolescence than the New Year's celebration. If we think how disconcerting it is when furniture is moved – how frustrated, foolish and at a loss we can feel when habitual movements, based on expectations of the old order, result in stumbling over obstacles or reaching into empty space – then we know how the adolescent feels as his internal world shifts. How much more so when the shape of his 'room' changes as well.

The mourning aspect of adolescence accounts for their sad and wistful moods, but their ebullience and vigour come from discovering and using the gains of the transition. Despite any reluctance to give up the old, it is actually difficult to resist the relentless forward push from physical, psychological and social forces, so the chief question for the young person is how to pace the progress in order to avoid feeling driven or overwhelmed. Curiosity and phantasy both help in different ways to make them masters of their own lives. What each individual can make of his apparently boundless present and future is dependent to a large extent on his past; it is no more realistic to assume that everyone will do justice to his opportunities than to assume that anyone can become prime minister. A more, or less, advantageous social position does affect what people can and can't do, but their curiosity and their conscious and unconscious phantasies about their opportunities and constraints matter more because these determine what they will and won't do. (Of course, the capacity to be curious and to engage in phantasy is already affected by past experience as well.)

CURIOSITY

Curiosity is a broad term with many meanings, but here it is used to denote an eagerness to learn. Inventions, discoveries, explorations, studies and new developments in every field begin with the glint of curiosity. Just as technical progress relies on someone wondering or asking why, so individual development is dependent on our wanting to know more about ourselves and our world. *Wanting* to know is the important thing: it is the safeguard against both complacency and the shock of having knowledge or experience forced upon us. By wanting, we retain the initiative and exert some control over what happens to us, and we give ourselves the excitement of the search and its rewards.

Young people have much to find out about themselves and the world, but this inevitably involves taking risks: if they are to be enticed by what they can't see or don't know, then they have to take their chances on meeting conflict, failure, confusion and disappointment as well as success and excitement. How predisposed and confident they are about following their inquisitiveness and taking risks depends on the response to their curiosity as a child, their sense of inner security, and their assumptions about the hazards of the external world.

Parents of small children react in different ways to curiosity - to the interminable 'Why?' questions, the dismantling of objects to see how they work, and bodily explorations. Some free their children by encouraging such activity, but others induce inhibition, shame or guilt by showing impatience or disapproval. Disparagement or amusement at a child's investigations and explanations can leave the child feeling odd and embarrassed or can subvert the purpose from discovery to entertainment. Overly intrusive interest in what the child is up to may result in a passion for secrecy and privacy where the fruits of curiosity are carefully, and often guiltily, guarded. For the child, exploration which ends in disaster - physical or interpersonal - is likely to make him think twice before risking such pain and bewilderment again: 'Once burned, twice wary.'

In a more general sense, a child's sense of inner security and his assumption that the external world is benign and trustworthy are fostered by his parents' capacity to expose him gradually to the diversity, demands and dangers of life, while protecting him sufficiently against anxiety and distress. Ideally they widen the child's world at the rate at which he can cope with it, either naturally or through their instruction. Over- and under-exposure to experience can both impair curiosity, either by associating change and exploration with fear and failure, or by implicitly conveying that the world is too dangerous or arid to deserve attention. Even those who are recklessly intrepid are actually not being truly curious; they are more likely trying to convince themselves that they are not afraid rather than wanting to know themselves and their environment.

Risk-taking, both physically and emotionally, means giving up a degree of control over known circumstances and abandoning fixed assumptions in order to be open to the freshness of what might be discovered. Because the attitudes and expectations about curiosity and safety are carried along from childhood and affect the degree of adventurousness and flexibility in the adolescent, such venturing is possible and profitable for those who can make 'educated guesses' about their situation: they have learnt enough about their resources and limitations and enough about the nature of the world to push the limits and avoid peril. They have enough certainty and trust to believe that, whatever happens, they will gain more than they might lose from trying something new. A musical analogy comes to mind: variations on a theme are exciting because the theme is firmly established, because virtuoso experimentation and diversity are held by the sustaining and structuring line and rhythm. Listeners are pleased by the daring of the music because they know it won't get out of hand and will ultimately resolve itself to the initiating phases. The link with the need to maintain continuity through change is obvious.

However, because curiosity is about gaining control as well as about knowing, it has a significant role in helping individuals manage fear. Probing the physical and emotional environment, inside and outside, at their own pace enables children to develop awareness and skills which they can rely on in new and unfamiliar circumstances. Now an analogy comes from fiction. We are thrilled but not frightened by the chances a long-running hero like James Bond takes because we know he will still be alive at the end, regardless of the content of his adventures. The feeling is quite different with one-off stories: instead of wondering what will happen next, we begin to worry about our hero – is he going to get out alive?

In so far as the young person can feel and be curious, and has an equal measure of reasonable fear, he can be enticed by the unknown with impunity. It is, after all, mostly through being unprepared that the unpredictable becomes unmanageable. For the already uncertain adolescent, however, such experimentation and investigation expose him to yet more uncertainty, and if often seems too much; excitement is sacrificed in the interests of simply surviving. Instead of wanting to find out, and to master, these overwhelmed people may resort to saying, through words or behaviour, 'I don't know' or 'I can't know'; or they exempt themselves by saying 'I already know' and 'It's not worth knowing.'

Career guidance is an area of counselling that highlights the importance of curiosity. A career decision is based on what you know of yourself so far and how you project yourself into the future, taking into account talents, preferences and needs. It is heavily influenced by assumptions and anxieties about the future which are significantly linked to the past, and these in turn determine how adventurous and flexible the options are. The fact that initial decisions are made during a phase of high ambiguity simply makes the decision process more complex and formidable.

> Arlene was about to leave school, having decided not to go to university, but she couldn't make up her mind about what to do. She had lived all over the world (because of her father's job), had studied many things, and had had a variety of interests. Despite the apparent scope of this, she had narrowed things down to a job in the country, not 9-to-5, not with animals, not scientific, and she wanted to be her own boss. She had great faith in her daily horoscope.

Her requirements were patently unrealistic, and her inflexibility seemed to be a consequence of continually thwarted curiosity. Because of their many moves, she had never been able to sustain projects and relationships, so she was good at starting things but had no confidence in her ability to follow them through. The moves also meant that she had had very little chance to make significant decisions based on her needs and preferences. She had given in to a belief that decisions only descend from higher powers like the government or the stars. In addition to this life-style, her mother was 'always too busy' and her father 'knew everything already', so she never felt that what she did was new and exciting. Feeling so powerless and insignificant in all spheres, she had lost interest even in herself. The changeability of the family life had invaded this girl, killing off any belief in her own initiative and teaching her to defend against loss and incompletion by not allowing herself to be emotionally committed. She did things mostly to fill in time, not to explore her world. It was, perhaps, her frustration that brought her to counselling – frustration about actions that couldn't be carried through, as well as a growing anxiety that this lifetime of opportunities would turn out to be a handicap unless she found out where *she* was and what impact *she* could have. Her job specifications indicated a wish to be free from all constraints and dependency.

Brendan represents the other end of the spectrum. While Arlene was over-exposed to life and not sufficiently protected, he was under-exposed and too greatly protected.

> Brendan didn't have a clue about what he wanted to do. In fact he positively didn't want to do anything – why should he? He was fanatically interested in canals but he had no intention of spoiling a hobby by making it a job, and nothing else was the least bit interesting. It emerged that the most attractive thing about canals was lying in a boat drifting along, gazing up at sky and trees which gave an ever-changing view without his even having to move his eyes.

Brendan's parents had worried over him, anticipated and satisfied every need, and had given way to any signs of conflict. Even now, desperate and angry as they were about him, they couldn't defend themselves against his taunting accusation that he hadn't asked to be born, and since they started by giving him life they should continue to do so. The relationship between them was a tragic irony. The parents had had to struggle for everything, and they were determined that their son would never see that toughness of life. Their struggle was increased by the relentless demands of the son, and they tired themselves out trying to gratify him. Brendan could find nothing attractive about growing up and going out to work, since, from what he could see of that world in his parents, it was simply exhausting. Besides, he gathered from them that reality was unkind, and he couldn't tolerate the frustration of delayed satisfaction. He didn't know what he was missing because he couldn't be bothered to look, and he couldn't imagine there would be anything worth while out there anyway. Underneath this, and very evident in his taunts, lay a ferocious anger with his parents who had effectively robbed him of the essential need to struggle and search for what he wanted and needed, but he didn't want to know about his feelings either. In reality he had the muscles of an adult, in phantasy he had the omnipotent power of the baby, and if the two connected up the outcome would be, he feared, bloody murder. Such utter passivity seemed necessary to prevent disaster.

And a third example:

> Audrey came for counselling because she was confused and depressed. She had failed her 'A' levels, thereby disrupting her plans for going to university to study dentistry. She was vaguely aware that she was afraid of leaving home and taking up a responsible training, and this obscure worry had contributed to her exam failure. Bright and capable, she felt an abysmal failure at trying to grow up. She liked being at home but had set up an unsatisfactory situation of becoming vegetarian in a meat-loving household, so she found herself sitting at the table, eating a meagre meal she had to prepare for herself, envious of the meat-eaters who were cooked for and who seemed to be having an altogether more robust life. She further alienated herself by having an affair with a married man, which had to be kept secret. Having failed, she didn't know what to do next. She had temporary jobs, mainly domestic, which she was enjoying.

Audrey was deeply mourning her childhood. She had flung herself into this affair, which was supposed to be about life and creativity, as a defence against loss and depression. The dependence–autonomy conflict was played out in her eating arrangements, where she remained in the family circle but separate from the others. Becoming vegetarian expressed her feeling of deprivation at no longer being a child and having the delicious things in life. Her career choices – dentistry and physiotherapy – seemed to be determined by an unconscious need to make good the damage she felt she was doing by simply growing up. For her becoming adult unconsciously meant destroying, replacing and harming existing adults. Her parents would, she said, die if they knew about her affair and other activities. (That cliché, when stripped of its banality, does precisely express the adolescent's view that growing up is inherently aggressive and is unconsciously about murder.) She very much needed to have her life planned and structured, especially to have safety built in along with danger. Her father was a policeman and had continually warned her about the danger lurking outside home, and he had actually prevented her from exploring their city. Although she did occasionally disobey, the normal and exciting curiosity had not been sanctioned for her, and she feared that going out without a safe route and a clear destination was doomed to disaster, be it to the cinema or a career. Audrey's situation was clearly constrained by her anxieties and uncertainties, so she hadn't been open to opportunities within herself and her immediate environment. Feelings of destructiveness and guilt were too closely linked with the urge to widen her experience. She was a very talented girl who had a particular affinity for colours and textures, but the urgency of preparing herself to repent and repair damage had obliterated any ideas about straightforward creativity.

PHANTASY

In the last two examples the influence of unconscious phantasy on decisions and actions is evident. Phantasy is also a broad term and here includes both unconscious assumptions and conceptions and conscious day-dreams, plans and anticipations. Whereas the dimensions of our immediate environment can only be known by taking actions in it, the realm of the self can be explored by both phantasy and action: phantasy consists of what we imagine we could be and do if the world were our own creation; our actions tell us how we actually are. Actions often contain an element of testing out phantasy, and this makes the link with curiosity: benign phantasy can be tried out, but anxiety-ridden phantasy prevents exploration. Unfortunately, unconscious phantasy is usually elaborated around a notion of something horrific - both Brendan and Audrey, for instance, imagined that they damaged and destroyed others - and, in carefully avoiding it, actions are severely restricted. Even ideas are sometimes restricted when the mere thought of the imagined disaster rouses too much anxiety. In this Brendan and Audrey differ: for Brendan, the extremity of his inertia indicated the extremity of his anxiety, and he was too terrified even to contemplate his feelings. Audrey, however, was actively trying to do something about her phantasy by looking for work which restored damage, and she was relieved to be able to reveal the drive behind her choices. It was safe for her probably because, while her father scaremongered, he also demonstrated that destruction could be confronted and contained. It was unsafe for Brendan because his parents backed away from conflict, leaving him feeling that fight was unmanageable.

It is common for adolescents to weave phantasy around the

unconscious belief in omnipotence, and in their imaginations they achieve wondrous feats. This is necessary; it helps them feel unique and in control, a counterbalance to whatever feelings of helplessness and chaos they also have. At best these phantasies contribute to their idealism and optimism, to their passionate belief in some system which will cure the ills of the world, to their consuming involvement in religion, politics and philosophy. It urges them to study in order to master and explain their world. The search for meaning and the attempt to discover the limits of personal power and the sources of genuine gratification in these ways are invaluable so long as they don't get out of hand. Sometimes there are near misses:

> Melvin was preoccupied with the relationship between man and God. He was wild about the blues and spirituals and believed he was invulnerable as one of God's little children. He took to driving down treacherous mountain roads in the dead of night, blinded by tears of painful joy evoked by his own impassioned singing. Those who had to stand by and watch did indeed feel his survival was a miracle. Finally, and mercifully, he did crash but sustained no injuries. He also was immensely relieved to have at last proved that he wasn't omnipotent and could stop that act of madness.

Sometimes there are painful disappointments when reality and phantasy become confused:

> Tom was a promising young scientist whose first class degree enabled him to go on for a PhD. He cherished the dream of being a super-scientist, and his research was the pioneering sort which could have made this come more or less true. But seven years after gathering his data, he still hadn't been able to write it up: the research had flaws in it which the super-scientist couldn't bear to put his name to. During the intervening years his work had been superseded anyway. Instead of being that super-scientist, indeed because of that phantasy, he was stuck in a mundane job.

Sometimes there is futility when ideas become a substitute for life:

> Andrew had been the nominal head of his family for eleven years since his father's death when he was thirteen. He'd also been around

the world, picking up whatever menial work he could, and had just finished a degree in sociology. His favourite word for other people was 'ridiculous' and his relationships were all tainted with anger and contempt. He wrote letters to newspapers and organizations incessantly, complaining about unsatisfactory service or monstrous social problems which could easily be solved with a little of his intelligence. But he couldn't get a job, and he never instituted any reforms. People were rude to him, he thought, but it never occurred to him that the problem might lie within himself.

Sometimes the phantasies can be exploited. In *Mystics and Militants* (1972), Adam Curle gives a masterly exposition of the young person's search for identity, and shows how his enthusiasm can be captured by the leaders of militant or mystical movements which seek radical change or Nirvana as means of establishing certainty. His argument can be extended to demonstrate the role of omnipotent phantasy. Militants act on the basis of their illusion that they can create a world according to their specifications for gratification of needs and wishes. Mystics conversely attribute the omnipotence to some greater magical force which they wish to merge with in order to eliminate their needs and wishes which are automatically provided for. One denies the old dependency; the other glorifies it. Both, so long as they are temporary, can be useful, but the phase has to come to an end when the phantasy can no longer stand up to the evidence of reality, as it did for one 'mystic' who sought her Nirvana in the Christian God: 'The trouble with God,' she regretfully conceded, 'is that He can't put His arms around me.'

The more conscious imaginative elaborations lie somewhere between make-believe and reality, and function like trial runs for actions and feelings which are strange or frightening. It has already been noted how bodily exploration and stimulation are private preparations for later physical and sexual encounters. Phantasy serves much the same purpose in helping to iron out 'mistakes' and awkwardness before the real thing happens. Most of us have probably completely rehearsed a difficult interview the night before and have imagined what we would do in even the most unlikely circumstances, like winning the pools or surprising a burglar, just in case that should happen. It allays anxiety by increasing our sense of being in control.

Susan and David had decided to marry, but they couldn't imagine what it would be like. One night on a long journey on the underground they spontaneously acted out a number of interactions - the amorous couple, the nagging wife, the male chauvinist husband, boring domestica. At the time the drama was simply fun, but in retrospect they were alarmed at how unpleasant they could be to each other. Forewarned is forearmed.

As a means of familiarizing ourselves with our feelings and ideas, phantasy is often crucial. Once they have become integrated and seem consistent with our self-image, then perhaps they can be tried out in the presence of others. Others, of course, are incorporated into our phantasy as we try to predict how they will react to us and how we shall respond to them. The difficulty here is that we tend to assume that others will behave more or less as we do, so we are disconcerted when, in reality, they behave quite differently. It is still fine to be taken by surprise, but phantasy aims, not always successfully, to protect us against humiliation and consternation.

Jonathan's father was coming from abroad and planned to spend a week with his son. He couldn't recall being alone with his father for more than a few hours at a time and was worried about the visit. Since his father had no friends here and spoke very little English, he imagined father would be helpless and dependent, much as he was when he first arrived here. To complicate matters, friends were also coming at the same time, and he had work to finish. He was very torn between having a good time with his friends, attending to his father, and completing his work. Underneath this obvious conflict, he was trying to sort out what kind of father he would be - would he be like his own father who was too busy with work and hobbies to spend time with his son, or would he be a better father who gave up his interests for a while? He imagined that Father would feel angry and deprived - exactly as he had - if he was ignored, so Jonathan planned several amusements for them together. Father was not pleased; in his customary self-contained manner he had made his own plans. Jonathan was hurt and felt unbearably foolish for planning what he hoped to happen, ignoring what he knew about his father.

Less exposing forms of phantasy occur in reading and writing. Books invite the reader into someone else's imaginative world, but it gives him a chance to see how others react and to test himself against them. Frequently, however, a story becomes a springboard for personal day-dreams. Certainly creative writing is often a vehicle where the young person can explore personal themes, becoming the hero of his own drama or working out pain and confusion. Putting it all down on paper involves capturing the material in the first place, and the writing becomes a symbolic realization of a day-dream or imposes structure on experiences which had previously eluded the writer. Diaries and journals are also used to capture and reflect on experiences and states of mind, but they have the additional purpose of being a private, fixed reference point to which the writer can return to remind himself of how he was then. With so much changing all the time, the permanence of the diary entry is a much needed reassurance that continuity exists.

RECAPITULATION

The need to hold on to personal continuity takes us back to the beginning: adolescence as a transition phase during which childhood has to be yielded to make way for adulthood, but in such a way that the present incorporates the past and anticipates the future. To recapitulate: reluctance to give up the old, because it is comfortabe and familiar, battles with a readiness to give it up, because it is too limiting; eagerness for the future, because it holds exciting possibilities, is set against fear of the future, because it is uncharted territory which naturally instils awe. As the individual encounters these conflicting pulls, his internal images and forces shift and his behaviour and relationships alter correspondingly.

Counselling shares many significant features of this transition process. Impetus for change comes from feeling limited or frustrated by how things are, but anxiety about giving up familiar patterns and using untested resources make movement forward tentative; confusion and contradiction are inevitable. Healthy curiosity is a necessary sustaining force and a willingness to explore day-dreams and worries through phantasy in order to reconcile them with reality is crucial. When these two are present, personal insight can be experimented with in reality and thus bring about enduring and genuine change.

2 ‖ The framework: theory

There is a myth that counsellors are born, not made; either they can do it naturally or they can't. Another myth maintains that all human problems are amenable to simple common sense; there is no need for a special category of therapeutic agents. Counselling, however, is neither magical nor mundane. The myths do not take account of the hard work of preparation behind the actual therapeutic hours, the competence in theory and technique which invisibly disciplines the counsellor's work. A counsellor has to establish a relationship which is firmly based in the reality of the everyday world but yet suspends reality enough so the client can explore himself and take emotional risks in a way he has never before dared. Within that relationship she listens to her client's communications and assimilates the messages to discover something new and illuminating. How she establishes that relationship and understands the communications depends on her theory - her ideas about how people develop and how things can go so awry that the individual ends up seeking help.

We are, however, understandably chary about theoretical structures because the last thing a client needs is to be boxed into a category or peered at as a textbook example: each person is, after all, unique and deserves better than that. Furthermore, pure theory is often couched in icy words and abstractions which seem ridiculous when applied directly to a living, moving person. It is fashionable in some quarters now to reject the concept of emotional disturbance by dismissing the notion of patients and the traditional nomenclature of pathology, thrusting the 'blame' on society, turning notions of sanity and madness upside down, and encouraging people to 'discover' themselves in intense groups open to the psychologically strong and vulnerable alike. The attempt to de-stigmatize emotional problems is laudable, but nothing is usefully served by trying to sidestep the fact that some people know that something is frighteningly wrong within themselves. They need to be taken seriously in that feeling: 'patho' does after all mean suffering or passion, as well as disease. Failing to attend to the distress usually makes things worse, and failing to place the distress in a personal context can result in more confusion.

BASIC PREMISES OF PSYCHOANALYTIC THEORY

We don't need theory as a collection of esoteric ideas or a set of rigid labels, but we do need it as a guide for the journey through the emotional maze laid out by the client: it's pointless for two people to get lost in it. When we meet a client we ask ourselves the question: 'Why is this person in this state now?' Theory primes us with a set of ideas about the nature of man and his relationships, ideas which help us to organize and make sense of what the client says about himself and his state. This book is based entirely on psychoanalytic ideas, specifically on the 'Object-Relations' school embodied in the work of Klein, Winnicott and Guntrip. The theoretical literature of psychoanalysis is vast and detailed, often making it difficult to see the wood for the trees. What follows is an attempt to abstract some premises of psychoanalytic theory, presented in a series of simple statements. Together they provide reference points which can be held in mind (without taking up the whole of it) when actually working with clients.

Each individual is the product and author of his own particular history: how he is now is a direct consequence of his earliest experiences with others and his environment. Subsequent experience confirms or modifies that early experience, for better or worse. He is not, however, passive in his history, but contributes to its shape.

He lives simultaneously in his external and internal worlds: the former he is mostly aware of, but the latter is primarily unconscious. The unconscious, internal world is energetic and substantially determines his feelings and actions in the external world.

All behaviour, no matter how apparently irrational and senseless, is logical and purposeful according to some personal system.

Chronological growth is inexorable, but emotional growth is beset by anxieties and detoured by defences and so doesn't always keep pace. Emotional disturbance is likely to be caused by some outdated and no longer appropriate motivation, decision (defence) or wish.

These statements are simple, but interrelated, so perhaps it makes sense to begin expanding them where we begin with a client: with the problem.

THE DYNAMICS OF SYMPTOMS

The 'healthy' personality is a dynamic system, changing continuously as the individual relates to others, to intentions, to events, to himself. He has to be ready to cope with his fluctuating and evolving circumstances, and he has a variety of mechanisms available to help maintain a degree of equilibrium. Obviously, that means that even the healthy person is in a state of disturbance – that is what keeps us alert, alive, interesting – but this necessary tension is relatively imperceptible, even pleasurable. When the equilibrium cannot be maintained because change is not keeping step with time, or because the mechanisms are not effective, the disturbance becomes noticeable and unpleasant, and becomes a problem or a symptom.

When asked why he is seeking help, a client will usually detail his symptoms – he will describe the signs, events or feelings by which he recognizes that something is wrong. According to psychoanalytic theory, the symptom (or problematic behaviour and feelings) contains a gold-mine of information about the client: it reflects his compromise solution to what he perceives as an intolerable situation; it incorporates a 'statement' about his interpersonal relationships; it reveals the level and extent of disturbance; and, in so far as the client is complaining, he is expressing either dissatisfaction with the compromise solution or anxiety that the defensive solution is breaking down and the original intolerable situation is emerging again.

Henry came for counselling on the eve of his twenty-first birthday, complaining of depression and anxiety about travelling on the underground, and saying 'If only I didn't have these problems, I'd be OK.' He had become depressed just before his 'A' levels. His school record was good, and he was expected to try for university entrance, but he wasn't sure about university – it sounded exciting and he'd like to get away from a difficult home situation, but no one in the family was educated and perhaps he couldn't look after himself. As he talked, he surprised himself into recognizing that leaving the security of home (where he had none the less felt deprived and resentful because his ill sister received all the attention) for the unknown of university was a substantial threat (and meant giving up any chance of being looked after). The unconscious anxiety interfered with his studying and exam performance, so he failed the entrance requirements. Now he was safe again. He took a job well below his level of competence, yet could only just manage it. His boss encouraged him toward promotion, but he developed 'trouble talking to people' which ensured no advancement. His situation was boring but tolerable because there was still no danger of growing out of the parental home. The recent trouble started when he noticed a middle-aged man at work – a distinctly odd man who still lived with his mother – and it occurred to him that he too could end up like that. Then he began to get panicky on the underground. He thought people were looking at him as if there were something abnormal about him. His friends teased him about not having a girlfriend (because of his trouble talking to people), but he couldn't think of anything else that would make him abnormal or odd.

Henry's depression was his compromise solution to an intolerable predicament. He wanted to make something of his life: he wanted to study, have a career, a girlfriend, but doing any of these meant moving away from home, both physically and emotionally, and that was 'dangerous'. It meant abandoning hope for parental attention, and, furthermore, he felt he needed to be an unadventurous and helpful son to his anxious mother, who had openly interpreted his wish to leave as a callous rejection of her. So he sacrificed university and instead took a job with prospects, but the same conflict between staying and leaving kept him from promotion. The compromise of trying but having problems which prevented success worked, and his depression was tolerable until the man at work confronted him with the consequences of such an existence. The emergency defence of trying to disown the feeling of oddness by putting it in the 'eyes' of the people on the underground only made him more panicky. It was impossible now to avoid confronting the original anxieties stirred at 'A' level time, which he did, eventually gaining promotion, moving into a flat with his mates, and at least talking to girls.

Henry was afraid he was having a breakdown. This message, the often-met fear of 'going mad', is straightforward. It means that there was an earlier, catastrophic event, or unconsciously imagined disaster, which was coped with by certain defensive moves, but those defences are no longer working, and they are faced with the original disaster all over again. The feared breakdown is the one they have already had. With Henry, the problem at 'A' level time was a repeat of an earlier crisis which had occurred when he was three when his little sister fell seriously ill, and he had had to grow up rapidly because his mother was preoccupied with the baby and needed his support. The 'growing up' was, however, spurious, a denial of his unmet needs, grief and resentment which all threatened to resurface at exam time, and again at the symbolic threshold of maturity.

It is likely that Henry had a good start in life with satisfying relationships which ended too abruptly. He had experienced and had then lost something – rather than never having had it at all – and he was still seeking to recapture that dependent relationship. Chronologically he was ready for independence, but emotionally he wasn't. The therapeutic task was to help his emotional age catch up with his chronological age by helping him to mourn and let go of the particular lost relationship so that he could be free for other relationships. When he could find in himself the child who had been lost in the activity surrounding his sister's illness, he was in a position to start growing up again as the alert and active person he had been before.

Henry's story demonstrates how disturbance results from the effects of outdated and inappropriate wishes and defences, which put emotional development out of step with chronological growth. It also shows how a current problem can be traced to its historical origins, and this leads back to the first of the basic premises of psychoanalytic theory.

BEING THE PRODUCT AND AUTHOR OF OUR HISTORY

This first statement, that each individual is the product and author of his own history, that how he is in the present is a direct consequence of his cumulative experiences which he in turn has consciously and unconsciously shaped, is manifestly obvious. At the social level, growing up in the city or on a farm, as the child of poor or wealthy parents, from an intact or broken home, in a criminal or religious subculture, all predispose us to regard money, honesty, the weather, ambition, food, free will, grandparents, and so on in quite specific ways throughout life. More personally, over time we accumulate ideas about ourselves and our environment, which lead us to have expectations about how we will interact with the world, and these expectations ultimately influence the interactions. We might, for instance, depend on feeling uncomfortable when meeting someone for the first time, so it doesn't surprise us when it happens, but we might not be aware that expecting to feel uncomfortable actually makes us anxious, therefore ensuring that we do feel uncomfortable and thus perpetuating the expectation. Similarly, when we review our lives we observe patterns in the way we go about life. We might see, perhaps, that we always reach the final of a competition, but we never win it, nor do we ever actually succeed in anything when it comes to the crunch. We know this is how it is because it has always been like that, and we plan and prepare accordingly, again making sure, inadvertently, that the pattern is repeated and confirmed.

Sometimes we think we know why we behave, think or feel as we do. We tend to simplify our history, recalling a single traumatic or unforgettable event somewhere in our past which explains everything that went wrong later; but it is seldom as simple as that. Experience is cumulative; the repetitive minutiae of daily interchange in our early years leave a more enduring mask than traumas do. When clients relate an incident which appears to be the precipitating cause of a problem, we are likely to discover that this event is a later version of some infantile anxiety or conflict arising out of how they were handled and how they responded when very young. Usually (but not always - sometimes there are genuine traumas which alter life radically), the vivid incident epitomizes a sort of relationship repeatedly experienced.

Sally came for help because, by the age of twenty-two, she had had no sexual interest or experience, but now she had a boyfriend and felt anxious and lost. To explain her problem she recalled, with burning shame, that when she was thirteen, she had skipped into the living room, wearing a pretty dress and swinging a new red handbag, happy and pleased with herself. Her father snapped that she looked like a whore.

For Sally that event was traumatic and put an end to any enjoyment of her femininity. Yet the incident crystallized, rather than created, her anxiety, and it reflected a general atmosphere that had always existed in the home. Sexuality was avoided verbally and physically: no one touched anyone else; the 'facts of life' came upon her unexplained; bodies were denigrated and covered up in drab garments; feeding and bath-time were business-like affairs, devoid of games, pleasure and bodily contact. In the handbag incident she was celebrating her pleasure in her physical femininity, but her father attacked both her sexuality and her pleasure, thereby confirming a persistent family view that such things are bad.

When we say, then, that the individual now is the product and author of his own history, we are speaking not just of simple events but of a continuing dynamic interaction through time at both conscious and unconscious levels. To understand this interaction, since what happens at one stage influences all subsequent stages of emotional development, we need to start at the very beginning of life. We need to look at what happens to the infant, his feelings about what happens, and the emotional significance he gives to people, events and feelings, because these three factors together make the major contribution to later characteristic patterns of living.

Babies cannot, of course, tell us about themselves directly, so much of psychoanalytic theory is formulated from inferences drawn from observations of infants and from adults' memories and dreams about their very early years. Adults do not ordinarily have access to these primitive experiences, even though they may sense or recognize the echoes in current activity, so the psychoanalytic focus on the dynamics of the beginnings of life often seems alien, unnecessary and excessively speculative. Those approaching the theory for the first time sometimes find that they need to suspend disbelief (if not indignation) temporarily in order to comprehend its content before they can see its relevance to what they feel and observe in themselves and others.

When a baby is born he is primarily concerned with what is happening in his own body - his physical needs and tensions. No longer in a state of biological unity with his mother, he is hungry, thirsty and cold for the first time, and his sole object is to satisfy these needs. It is a question of survival: without food and warmth he will die. Although initially he is not aware of discrete people and things in the world around him, still he seeks from the beginning to find this satisfaction through relationships in phases of increasing discrimination and awareness. The first phase is a 'global' one where he and his environment are totally undifferentiated and all is entirely benign or malign, depending on whether or not he is satisfied and safe. Gradually he perceives that food and warmth aren't totally present or absent and are also separate from him, so having them requires something in his mouth or something holding him. These things – his mother's breast or arms – are then all-important as the sources of survival and pleasure, and his first relationship is with these feeding and holding parts of his mother. (The rest of her doesn't yet count in his system, and won't, until his memory and perception develop so he can encompass her as a whole person.) If these necessary parts are there when he needs them, he is satisfied and safe; if they are not, he is tense and endangered. The second stage is characterized by 'either-or': either the goodies are there or they aren't, either he is safe or he isn't. Whichever state obtains, he believes it will last for ever. The third stage is the 'sometimes' phase, and comes when the baby's perception and memory allow him to know that sometimes the goodies are there and sometimes they aren't, sometimes he is safe and sometimes he isn't, but things can and will change.

So far we have been talking of the basic events and people in almost mechanical interchange. If we now add feeling about what happens, the interaction becomes immediately more complex. The baby wants to survive – as shown by his assertive demand for food and warmth – and we speculate that he wants to be loved. If his physical needs are meet his wishes to survive and be loved are gratified, and he feels content and excited; failure in satisfaction brings anxiety and despair. The mother brings a more involved set of feelings to the relationship, based on her own experience of other babies and herself as a baby and her current environmental and emotional state. If she has favourable images of babies and is mostly free from other external responsibilities and internal anxieties, she will be able to give her baby the good and satisfying experiences he needs and wants, but if she is harassed, uncertain, depressed or afraid, these will get in the way and leave the baby anxious and fearful. Mother and baby intuitively pick up each other's feelings, and reactions and counter-reactions reverberate between them. The baby, who on the whole enjoys his natural aggression and is with a mother who is free to give herself over to him so that both find the relationship gratifying and exciting, has a radically different basis for his life from the baby who is restless and is with a busy or distraught mother, so that both find the relationship anxious and unsatisfying.

Theresa had long wanted a baby but couldn't believe that she could actually have a healthy baby. Unfortunately, although this wasn't discovered immediately, her baby wasn't perfectly healthy, and he cried relentlessly. The more he cried, the more scared Theresa became, and the more panicky the baby became. After a couple of days at home and after one particularly unsuccessful attempt at feeding, Theresa took him back to the hospital, disappointed, guilty and terrified. She gave him back to the nurse, saying she didn't want him any more. The nurse, not already caught up in the vicious circle, was able to calm the baby and see that something was physically wrong. Theresa eventually took him back, but their relationship remained an anxious one.

Finally, to arrive at a full understanding of the interaction, we need to consider the emotional significance (the 'interpretation') given to the events and feelings in the relationship. In the example just given, Theresa brought from her own early experiences anxiety about being a 'bad' mother who could only produce a damaged baby. Paradoxically, when faced with a truly ill baby, she dismissed as irrational the conviction that her worst fears had come true. Eventually, however, her frustration with him led to anger and the fear that she would kill him, so she had to protect them both by giving him to the nurse. The child, apparently sensing his mother's fear and guilt, behaved as if he were afraid of her. All of this was, of course, unconscious.

It is difficult enough to understand the unconscious significance given to a situation by adults; but probably no one who has observed babies will deny that they have 'ideas' about what is going on and that they react according to these ideas. Certain kinds of idea seemed to be linked specifically with each of the three phases.

In the first 'global' phase, the baby imagines in an omnipotent way that simply because he is, for instance, hungry he has 'created' the food. The whole world and its food are part of himself. Natural frustration of his needs and wants helps him to understand that the world and its food are separate from him. This brings him to the second 'either-or' phase, but he is still so much under the sway of omnipotent phantasies that he imagines he makes the feeder come when he wants her. By the same token of omnipotence, however, when the feeder doesn't come, he imagines that he has done something to keep her away from him. The frustration then makes him angry and afraid, partly because the pain of hunger is hurting him and making him worry about surviving and partly because his omnipotence seems to have become bad. Because he cannot tolerate feeling so bad, he magically short-circuits his anger by denying it within himself and attributing it to the feeder. But now he becomes afraid of this feeder who he feels is angry with him and apparently wants to starve him.

In this 'either-or' phase in the baby's mind, the experiences and people around him are rigidly categorized in black and white terms. There are several permutations of these splits and they shift according to the balance of alarm and anger. For instance, there is the ideally good feeder who satisfies him, and the equally bad feeder who stays away and would starve him; there is the good baby who gets fed, and the bad baby who deserves starvation; there is the wholly good relationship between the perfect feeder and baby, and the wholly bad relationship between the persecuting feeder and the hateful baby; there is the relationship of the perfect feeder with the bad baby (who daren't 'spoil' his feeder with his anger because he is dependent on her for survival), and the evil feeder and innocent baby (who can't bear acknowledging his bad feelings lest he is rejected because of them). These divisions, which are based on an omnipotent allocation of feelings, are absolute until, with the help of his mother who enables him to tolerate his anxiety and anger, he can move into the third 'sometimes' phase and realize that there aren't two separate situations: the same mother sometimes satisfies and sometimes frustrates, and the same baby sometimes feels content and loved and sometimes feels frightened and hateful.

The third phase of relating, although more realistic, arouses yet other phantasies and interpretations. Having recognized the wholeness and autonomy of his mother, he has to cope with his loss of omnipotent control and take account of her needs as seen by him through her actions. Most crucially, he has to come to terms with feeling love and hate towards someone who is at once lovable and hatable. Vestiges of omnipotence linger in his inability to distinguish clearly between thought and action, and his feelings are still *in extremis*. When he focuses his anger on some aspect of her, he is still prey to anxiety about harming or killing her, but his alarm now is not only that he will not survive her rejection or retaliatory attack, but also that he has hurt someone he loves and who doesn't deserve his attack. Guilt and concern follow, and he tries to deal with them by trying to make good the damage he imagines he has done. If she can accept his attempts at reparation for what they are, his guilt is assuaged, and he is reassured about his capacity for genuine concern and creativity. If, however, his anxiety and guilt are not relieved by timely and adequate responses, he must do something to get rid of the intolerable feelings. 'Doing something' means invoking a defence which will bring about an imagined satisfactory resolution to the unbearable situation. By now many defences are available to him, and the one he chooses is determined by his interpretation of his circumstances. For example, if it seems that no one will feed him and his anger feels too dangerous, he may deny his needs, as if to say: 'If I'm not hungry, then I won't feel angry or afraid. I'll just wait and be grateful if some food comes my way.' Or he may decide to become equally 'nasty' and actively spoil the relationship by spitefully refusing whatever is offered despite needing and wanting it. (Both these patterns, which are only two among many possible ones, are easily recognized in the self-effacing or contemptuous adult.)

This way of conceptualizing the early relationships comes from the work of Melanie Klein (1959): the 'either-or' phase is her 'paranoid-schizoid position', and the 'sometimes' phase is her 'depressive position'. She obviously elaborates them in her writings, but here it is sufficient to note that these basic models of interactions, the accompanying phantasies and the defences are laid down like templates in the unconscious inner world to be used as ways of construing similar events - or ones which can symbolize them from that time onwards.

> Kate was by all accounts a robust and active baby. Her grandmother told her, rather accusingly, that she thrashed about so much that her mother couldn't hold her and had to put her down. When men now 'put her down', she believes they are weak and frightened by her liveliness. She's angry with them and feels guilty about being angry because it's 'her fault' that makes them weak.

To recapitulate: for the baby, from the first 'global' phase comes the idea that everything in the world is part of him and therefore under his omnipotent control; from the second 'either-or' phase comes the predisposition to divide himself, others and relationships into rigid and extreme categories in an attempt to retain absolute control over his experience; from the third 'sometimes' phase comes the recognition of himself and others as autonomous beings whose competing needs and mixed qualities need to be taken into account in relationships. Current behaviour and feelings are directly linked to early experiences through this process of interpreting the world according to these three basic models, although, of course, there are individual variations based on each individual's specific past and present circumstances.

The third phase reflects the true nature of people and the world and is consequently the most healthy. Some people, because of adverse conditions, may never reach this phase but remain stuck in an earlier one, others achieve it but may revert to earlier phases under stress. Getting stuck at any particular phase, or with any particular mode of gratification, usually means that one of two things has happened: if, on the one hand, the baby wasn't able to resolve anxieties attendant on that stage or never actually obtained the desired gratification in his relationships, then he is fixed there, hoping for gratification or resolution. If, on the other hand, gratification at one point was so satisfying, or the anxieties of the next stage so frightening, then it may seem altogether better to stay put. Sally illustrates this second case: apparently sexuality was so bad and dangerous that it was better for her to deny such feelings and to avoid venturing into that realm entirely. Theresa demonstrates the first point:

Theresa was sent for counselling because she practically lived in her GP's surgery, bringing an endless and rather imaginative series of complaints about her health. Referral to several specialists had failed to explain them or cure her. Even her indulgent husband was growing impatient with her ailments and her need for attention. Theresa was the middle of five children, and, because her father was frequently ill, her mother had little time and energy to go around. The siblings on either side of her paired together, so she was left without a special relationship and with an experience of genuine deprivation. Her life's purpose was to get what her childhood hadn't given her, and she therefore remained stuck at the level of a baby wanting special attention. Although she chose a method which had worked for her father – being ill – her efforts were doomed to failure. First of all, she wanted that specialness with her mother – doctors and husband wouldn't do. Secondly, her method repeated her original experience: there were always lists of patients on either side of her, so she never received undivided or unlimited attention. She thought of herself as an unworthy, unsatisfactory and demanding girl, so although she was secretly irritated by the long waits and the insufficient attention from the doctors, she felt she had no right to complain. Instead she worried about tiring and burdening them. Indeed, so much did she need to be the good, untroublesome child (whom mother would surely love), that usually by the time she saw the specialists her symptoms had disappeared. Although relieved that she wasn't actually asking for anything, she worried more about bothering such busy people about nothing. The final evidence of her being stuck in this obsolete pattern was that she really didn't see people as whole beings: for her they were either carers or non-carers, and she was very quick to detect, rightly or wrongly, any signs of their tiredness or irritation with her. This was, of course, unconscious. Theresa could describe her husband, mother, siblings and counsellor in completely real terms, but she related to them only in terms of how much energy and willingness they had to care for her.

Theresa's story shows how we are at once product and author of our own history: our early experiences leave us with certain unconscious constructions and expectations about later life, so we are the product of our history; but, in so far as we unconsciously attribute meaning to those experiences and actively impose those interpretations later, we substantially shape our own history.

THE UNCONSCIOUS

It will be evident by now that the concept of the unconscious is central to psychoanalytic theory, because it is so influential in determining how we manage our feelings and behaviour. Obviously the unconscious isn't a *lack* of awareness: it is a very positive, effortful phenomenon by which certain aspects of ourselves and our experience are disallowed to our conscious awareness, either because they are unacceptable or because they became ours by processes which are themselves unconscious.

Freud called the unconscious a seething cauldron, as if it were a repository for all the wishes, impulses and bits of ourselves which would be dangerous or anxiety-making if permitted a place in our conscious awareness: a motley collection of primitive, anti-social, unacceptable, or otherwise outrageous things, which we would prefer not to own as part of ourselves. So far it seems like a dustbin but, unlike the dustbin, no one comes along to empty it for us. The material relegated to it remains with us, active and turbulent. Furthermore, it's less a motley collection than an organized dynamic entity, a complete internal world with its own psychic reality. We tend to regard the unconscious with fear and apprehension, as something generally nasty, sneaky and embarrassing (when it turns up unexpectedly in dreams and verbal slips), but that is like declaring the whole unconscious guilty by association with *some* of its content, because the contents are not inevitably bad.

All sorts of things can be unconscious – impulses, wishes, drives, values, conflicts, aims, defences, images of people and the self and relationships. Objectively, nothing there is good or bad; such attribution arises out of our negative feeling about the force in question. We have already seen, for instance, how the frustrated baby's natural anger only becomes 'bad' when it is anxiously associated with his murderous intent. Different sorts of love will also be found in the unconscious if for some reason they were perceived as a threat when expressed toward a particular person. Any inter- or intra-personal feeling can become unacceptable once it arouses too much conflict or anxiety. It is then subject to the defensive processes of repression and denial which render it unconscious. Usually it is more specific, however, so that a particular feeling in a particular context or relationship has to become unconscious. We often meet clients, for instance, who are fully aware of their anger with everyone except their mother, and who will aver that they feel nothing but love for her. They resist knowing about that anger because it remains too dangerous to hate the powerful person on whom they were once so dependent.

The part of the unconscious which is made up of repressed, unacceptable or threatening feelings, aspects or images feels 'bad'. However, there are other ways of relegating material to the unconscious which do not necessarily carry negative overtones: through the process of internalization we take in and hold images derived from our interactions; and through identification we 'acquire' aspects of others which then become part of our internal and unconscious self.

We have already noted some of the images acquired through early relationships: an evil baby and starving mother, a needy baby and a mother who comes when needed, a weak mother and unmanageable child, an over-busy mother and an unworthy child. Throughout life we build up an infinite number of these images involving significant people and interactions, many of them partial and usually representing *patterns* of feelings and behaviour. They may be accurate representations of what actually occurred, or they may be distorted by the interpretation of what happened. Together, the images are organized into a kind of unconscious internal world which is psychologically as real as the external one, as present as current reality, and as powerful in determining action as conscious intentions.

INTERNAL AND EXTERNAL WORLDS

This internal world is not a static alternative to the external one, and there is constant interplay between the two: further experience may add to or modify the pre-conscious internal images, and the pressure from the truly unconscious forces can steer us into repeating early patterns. Consequently we live in the two worlds simultaneously. If the two are in harmony, we have no problems; but if our conscious and unconscious aims and wishes differ, we suffer conflict and confusion. The difference may result merely in surprise, or it may involve us in difficult and painful struggles. We can observe the surprise effect of minor differences in our day-to-day interactions. For instance, in relationship with our superiors we unconsciously expect to be praised or reprimanded by them in the ways that our parents used to praise or punish us, and are surprised if that doesn't happen. Or living with a chronically ill and grumpy grandparent throughout childhood may lead us to avoid elderly invalids and perhaps to have twinges of guilt when we discover that some are sweet-tempered and courageous. Such interactions may introduce new or modified internal images of people and relationships.

The consequences may be tragic, however, when more powerful and pressing forces are at work so that the balance is upset, and the unconscious dynamics dominate the conscious interaction.

Mark saw the world as a place where everyone was totally self-centred, and no one cared about him. Feeling left to struggle on his own, he'd made a virtue of self-sufficiency. His mother had been hospitalized sporadically for physical and emotional reasons during his early years and could only care for and about him during periods of respite. With one exception, his relationships with women repeated this pattern of episodic involvement; sometimes they were with women who couldn't care about him consistently, and sometimes instead he identified with his mother and cared about the women only when it suited him. Several of these encounters had resulted in pregnancy and abortions. The crunch came when one girl refused an abortion and insisted on marriage. Consciously he felt forced into marriage by her ultimatum, but he also unconsciously believed that at last he had found a woman who was interested in babies and would look after *his* hitherto neglected baby-self. She did indeed become utterly preoccupied with their real baby, and so Mark's baby-self was again neglected. He was resentful and depressed and jealously destroyed the plants she tended (thankfully not his baby son). He saw only that she cared about her own involvement with the baby and failed to see how she did care about him as a husband. He became impossibly demanding and scorned as inadequate whatever she did do for him. Eventually she gave up trying and actively went on strike, refusing to provide meals and clean clothes. By this time the marriage was a shambles, and he threatened to leave, just as, when a baby, he had emotionally 'left' his mother by denying his need and affection for her.

In Mark's case his unconscious took over, muddling up his external and internal world. Here in reality was an adult man marrying a woman; but here also was a baby seeking a willing mother within the very same relationship. The latter, unconscious relationship was by far the more important to him. He complained consciously that his wife didn't appreciate him - by which he meant that he slaved away to earn money, and she couldn't be bothered even to provide food or mend shirts. The underlying, unconscious complaint was that she didn't appreciate (understand) that he was more a baby than a husband. He in turn could see that she needed to be involved with their baby, but under the sway of his own infantile failure to appreciate the realities of the world, he couldn't emotionally tolerate or comprehend her maternal absorption any more than he had been able to comprehend what was happening to his own mother. His persistent, enraged, partial view of his wife (this 'my mother' doesn't care about this 'baby-me') which blanked out her appropriate husband-caring activity and ultimately drove her to withdraw, leaving him to fend for himself. Thus she confirmed his infantile image of women–mothers. (It is important to say that although the force of his need for confirmation of this image caused his wife to change, she had her own unconscious needs to satisfy in the marriage, so a collusion between them arose.) Needless to say, the disintegration of his marriage was all the more confusing and bewildering to him because he was utterly unconscious of his baby needs; indeed having made a virtue of self-reliance, because of his inability to cope with the anxiety caused by the inconsistent caring from his mother and his rage about it, he had denied his emotional need for another person.

Our unconscious world can make itself felt in a powerfully disruptive way, causing us to structure the real world according to dominant internal images, so that we are selective in what we perceive or in the sort of people we choose to relate to. When the boundary between the internal and external world gets blurred, we can misconstrue events and people in a disastrous way. The resultant confusion needs to be resolved, and one way to do this is by behaving in such a way that others will actually change in their behaviour towards us (as Mark's wife did), so the real world comes into line with our psychic world.

The force of such surfacing unconscious needs resides partly in their being infantile in origin. Relegating things to the unconscious usually has the effect of putting them into a time-capsule, sealed off from any interaction with subsequent experience and hence denied the opportunity for modification or change. The infantile extremity is thus preserved: the feelings or needs are still associated with the all-or-nothing, life-and-death struggle for biological and psychological survival. Paradoxically, the intensity is even more threatening when it emerges later because, while the baby was helpless at acting out his omnipotent phantasies, adults have the muscular capability to do just that. Unconscious material gains further spurious power simply because it is so markedly anachronistic – a characteristic which arouses anxiety in its own right. In the early Freudian system it was postulated that the strength of the unconscious came from its being locked behind the defensive barriers, pounding to get out, so that when it does breach the barriers, it does so like water rushing through sluice-gates. If we recognize the power of the accompanying anxieties, such a mechanistic explanation becomes unnecessary.

THE LOGIC OF THE UNCONSCIOUS

It might seem that disposing of unmanageable, threatening or unacceptable material into the unconscious sphere by repression should be a convenient dumping process, but that misses the central value of the process for the individual's psychological survival. When in real physical danger, the enemy doesn't vanish and we defend ourselves against the danger and cope with the anxiety by fleeing or fighting. The psychological process is exactly the same, with the major difference that the unconscious psychological enemies reside mainly in phantasy. As already noted, if an infant can stay with his anxiety and rage in frustrating situations long enough and often enough to experience the genuine reassurance of satisfaction, then after a while he need not defend himself against those feelings. In the absence of certainty that satisfaction will come (or in the actual absence of satisfaction), however, the infant makes, as it were, a short-term decision to put a stop to the immediate circumstances and to his immediate feelings. His subsequent relief is enough to confirm the validity of the 'decision' and predisposes him to invoke the defence again, or even to institute it as a permanent feature of his way of relating to the world. Such defensive manoeuvres are, of course, unconscious.

Although this emergency measure copes with the immediate situation, in the long term it has debilitating consequences. The very process which was once 'life-saving' prevents us from realizing other satisfactions. Defences entail the sacrifice of part of ourselves and the feelings and energy involved in what is being avoided. Consequently these are no longer available to us, and we are diminished by precisely those features. Furthermore, we lose the free use of the additional energy required to keep the defence operative. Suppressing the 'bad' bit of the unconscious is a tiring business – indeed, people seeking help will often complain of being chronically tired and depressed, meaning by 'depressed' that they are functioning at less than full capacity. Subjectively, it feels like carrying a heavy and awkward weight around all the time.

Loss of freedom is also an inherent consequence of a defensive manoeuvre – freedom to use all the possibilities of the self and the world, and freedom to make choices among opportunities. In order to take advantage of the richness of the world, we have to see what is there, we have to look around, be interested, curious and reasonably unafraid. The more we are fettered or blinkered by preoccupations and anxieties from the past, the less we can be in the present; the more we selectively perceive only those possibilities relevant to a particular need or relationship, the narrower is our experience.

We want to be able to make choices; we want to be our own agent, not driven by unconscious forces – neither impelled to repeat old patterns of relating nor to avoid situations that were once anxiety-making. Clients often complain that they are not running their own lives; they feel as if it is being run for them, or that external constraints prevent them from doing what they really want. At some level this is true. They are being run by unconscious forces which compel them to allow external factors to constrain them unnecessarily. The sense of helplessness arises not from the mere existence of the unconscious pressures, but from the attempt to disown and deny responsibility for them. Obviously we don't want to admit to the content of the 'bad' unconscious; if we did, it wouldn't be there. Somehow being a passive victim of that part of ourself is preferable to accepting and integrating it, no matter how distressing the victim-state is.

Living at the mercy of the dictates of the unconscious, or according to one of the anachronistic templates, or within the confines of a permanently erected defence means that we often do apparently senseless things or fail to make the most of our lives. Most clients are indignant at the suggestion that their particular problem for which they are seeking help was actively and deliberately (albeit unconsciously) chosen because having it seems better than what would happen if they didn't have it. Rather than see it as purposeful, they will say the problem is silly, burdensome and illogical; and so it may seem. The unconscious itself may be illogical, irrational, lacking in respect for ordinary time and space and otherwise chaotic, but within the total person it is systematic and relevant. Its manifestations may initially seem bizarre and bewilderingly out of place, out of date, contradictory and inappropriate, but historically it all makes sense: once upon a time there was a perfectly good reason for all things our unconscious makes us do, perfectly good, that is, in the psychological reality of that person at that time and in that situation.

Ezriel's (1963) formulation of this is highly graphic. He describes three interrelating relationships: the 'required', the 'avoided', and the 'catastrophic'. The 'required' relationship is the defensive one set up by the individual. It is required (necessary) in order to escape the 'avoided' relationship, which is the one where a troublesome need or impulse would be directly expressed. The individual actually *wants* the avoided relationship but daren't have it because it might end in 'catastrophe'. The catastrophe is some form of breakdown or damage (real or imagined). In Henry's case, he relates to people as 'depressed' or 'having trouble talking to people' (required relationships) because he daren't assert himself (the avoided relationship) because he might not survive on his own or might damage his mother (the catastrophes). Similarly, Sally is asexual because being sexual causes too much anxiety. Ezriel's formula isn't always the most useful one, but it does always apply. Mark and Theresa, for instance, may be more usefully understood as the child part of themselves tenaciously attempting to gain some satisfaction which has continually eluded them, but they are still caught in required relationships.

Helping people to let go of their required relationships, to give up their 'emergency' solutions which have become permanent ones, to know about their unconscious, or to forgo a futile struggle left over from the past – which are the tasks of counselling – is difficult precisely because these defences and childhood patterns have been, at some time, so useful, necessary and comforting. If the advantages didn't outweigh the disadvantages in some very significant way, it would be easy to change. When they come for counselling, our clients expose themselves to the terrifying prospects of re-experiencing awful anxiety or of depriving themselves of some long-cherished gratification, so it is hardly surprising that they drag their feet or retreat from the process from time to time. However, the fact that the unconscious isn't an emptiable dustbin, but can keep the anxiety-ridden feelings and images until they can be managed, means that freedom and choice can be retrieved; this is what encourages clients to come in the first place.

3 ‖ The framework: diagnosis

Because enduring change in behaviour involves alterations in the unconscious inner world and this threatens the client's defensive solutions to his anxieties, counselling is often slow, painful and resisted, so the counsellor needs to approach the process of change as effectively and parsimoniously as possible. The client and counsellor have to tackle the right problem at the right level, taking into account the time available for work and the client's motivation and emotional resilience. To do this they need to ask questions about the nature and degree of disturbance and to establish what sort of change is realistically possible. Is this a temporary hitch in a heretofore smooth development? Is this an immediate reaction to some recent experience? Is this a long-standing problem which is only now bothersome for some reason? Does it permeate his whole personality or does it affect only part of himself and his life? What strengths and resources does he have for withstanding the turmoil of change? What does he want for himself, and how much time and energy will he give to working for that? These are diagnostic questions, and the answers, no matter how tentative, point to what the counselling can or should encompass and how it might be achieved. It is obvious that a frail and isolated person in an acute crisis would need a different response from someone who is managing well enough but is fed up with a persistent nagging depression. But often the diagnostic process involves balancing ambiguous 'evidence' about the nature of the problem and finding ways of working in circumstances which are less than ideal in terms of time, setting, motivations and personal resources.

THE VALUE OF THE DIAGNOSTIC PROCESS

'Diagnosis' frequently arouses protests of indignation about labelling people as ill and treating them as impersonal objects. Such implications are not inevitable, but they seem to follow from our uneasy feelings about emotional problems. Sophisticated as we may be, an 'odd' person in the street still evokes a flicker of terror which is soothed by the thought that he is 'mad' and therefore different from us. This reassures us of our own 'normality' and we feel less frightened, but the relief is tainted by guilt because such thoughts haven't helped the other to be less disturbed and frightened. On the countrary, 'fixing' him as different arguably confirms and perpetuates his madness, and neither does justice to his complexity and individuality nor acknowledges our own potential to, or actual bits of, madness. From the other side, some people do label themselves in psychiatric terminology. Usually they have sunk into a negative pathological identity with some relief at having given up the struggle to make sense of their confusion in a less static way; 'knowing' in itself provides comfort. Labels, colloquial or scientific, therefore simultaneously contain the security of knowing and a defensive refusal to know, reassurance and guilt. The process of labelling is the pursuit of certainty, but it also contains disappointment because it produces unreliable and partial truths.

The diagnostic process, however, need not produce a label and certainly does not come to a halt with one. In fact, it is really an integral part of the total therapeutic process, and it depends for its validity on co-operative exploration by client and counsellor together. As the client talks about himself, the counsellor forms a tentative explanation or interpretation about what she hears and sees, which she puts to the client for him to consider, confirm or modify. This becomes the starting-point for the next formulation, and there is continual overlap between the interpretations directed at discovering where the problem lies and those working toward its resolution. Psychoanalytic theory readily lends itself to this diagnostic-therapeutic blend because it is descriptive in character and is immediately concerned with interpersonal relationships - current and historical, real and phantasied - and how those four come together in the problem experienced by the client. Both client and counsellor gain from interpretation: the client gets a new or clearer view of what he says and feels; the counsellor gains more information which leads to the next interpretation.

A condensed account of a first session with a running commentary of the counsellor's thoughts in brackets will perhaps demonstrate this:

Lucy complains of feeling depressed (but she looks and sounds irritable: depression is an omnibus word). The counsellor asks what 'depressed' means to her. She says she's bored, can't concentrate, isn't interested in work, can't be bothered to have a social life. ('Not concentrating' means she has distracting thoughts which are unacceptable, so she's bored?) In fact, after her last boyfriend, she's decided not to go out with men any more, but maybe that's not the right thing to do. (Dealing with a problem with men by avoiding them?) The counsellor asks about this relationship and with other men. Lucy describes three relationships, in all of which the men don't give her enough attention, fail to satisfy her sexually, and refuse to do the sexual 'tricks' she needs. She's disappointed, but asks if it's wrong to want to enjoy sex – women aren't supposed to. (Her relationships have a pattern. She's sure about what she wants, but her tone changes and the question is edgy, so perhaps she is feeling guilty and wrong?) The counsellor asks who says or said that women shouldn't like sex. She says that was how she was brought up; society says so. She vehemently mentions her commitment to a Women's Lib group. The counsellor suggests that her ideas and feelings about sex conflict – she seems to feel bad about it, but resents having to feel bad. Lucy denies feeling guilty but expands the Women's Lib theme to include other things women have a right to but men deny them. (Sex is a battleground for another problem of wanting more than she gets, which she's twice mentioned? Two themes now. Perhaps timing will tell us something.) The counsellor asks when all this started and gets a lengthy, highly charged reply. It began a few weeks ago, just after she'd returned home after a long absence. Her parents have just divorced and her father is now living with his second family of three young children and a woman not much older than herself. She stayed with them, but felt very uncomfortable. He obviously loves the children and lavishes affection on them. It's so nice that he is finally happy. He was too busy working to be a father to her when she was little. Mother is unhappy but stupid because she still works for father and has to see him happy without her. The counsellor suggests that she isn't really pleased about Father's new-found happiness, although she would like to be for his sake. Lucy defends her father, but this breaks down and eventually she expresses her resentment about his giving his new family the affection he didn't give her. (So the two themes come together: the sexual father who deprives the girl/woman of what she has a right to: affection and sex. Her depression probably expresses both her blocked anger towards her father who is represented by her boyfriend, the blockage due to guilt about jealously wanting the man who belongs to other women and children, and her humiliation at being rejected by him.) The counsellor suggests that she is depressed because she has to hide away her underlying feelings of anger and humiliation which are really connected with her wish for her father's love, a wish which is, in some senses, socially prohibited. This Lucy confirmed with the information that her relationships were with married men, but all she really wanted was to be fed and amused by them once she had attracted them with sex. Her sexual demands upset and bewildered her.

Despite the earlier emphasis on sexuality, Lucy's problems lay in the area of her anger about feeling deprived of love and affection and her uncertainty about what she could realistically and rightfully expect from others. This diagnosis proved central and stood the test of further information about her life and feelings; arriving at it in this fast-moving first session was clearly therapeutic in that her boredom vanished and her concentration returned immediately. Finding a satisfactory social life took months, however.

The psycho-dynamic approach to diagnosis through trying to locate the specific troublesome feelings and relationships and placing them in their historical context is, of course, only one way of formulating the nature of disturbance. Even within the analytic framework there are several slightly differing structures - Klein's paranoid-schizoid and depressive positions; Freud's oral-anal-genital stages; Ezriel's required and avoided relationships and catastrophe; Malan's (1979) trio of needs, anxieties and defences - but they all focus on significant relationships and have the practical advantage of telling us how the client arrived at his problem which is already a long step in the direction of resolution. The more medically based models focus on symptoms within the traditional scheme of normal, neurotic or psychotic. One formulation is that the differences are quantitative: the ordinary feelings of normal people are increasingly exaggerated down the scale, so that the obsessional checking of a severely debilitated person is the same, only worse, as the careful counting of banknotes by a teller. Another is that the differences are qualitative, so the distinctive features of psychosis, say hallucination, will not be found in a neurosis. The classification is only partially exclusive, however, so neurotic traits might be found in a psychotic. A third way is to consider what people do with their irrational anxieties: do they defend against them, do they act on them, do they treat the irrational as valid? In practice all of these are used in various mutations and combinations, depending on how the client chooses to present his problem, although these psychiatric models are less easily shared immediately with the client. With young people the task of understanding the level and focus of disturbance may be particularly difficult, so every possible way of looking at their problems is a welcome member of the diagnostic armoury.

ADOLESCENT DISTURBANCE: THE PERILS OF GROWING UP

Even the most 'normal' adolescent appears utterly incomprehensible and inconsistent from time to time, and these aberrations can look like serious disturbance. Their rapid mood changes, unpredictable outbursts, risky behaviour, and resorts to phantastical activity are the outward signs of their attempts to manage the resurgence of primitive anxieties and the stresses of loss and change. When they feel swamped, defeated or scared, even the fundamentally strong young people will appear extremely fragile and distressed.

Neil appeared at his GP's surgery a few days after sitting his finals and a few days before leaving home to start a good job. He was frightened and bewildered because recently he had been driving rashly, and the previous night had actually gone to the roof of a high-rise building intending to jump. He was fascinated by the image of being crushed. He was also having nightmares, all of which involved being lost in some desolate place and coming out of his wandering at cemetery gates. He remembered that he had been depressed after 'A' levels and had thought of taking an overdose but that had passed. Otherwise he thought of himself as psychologically all right. Both his parents were 'messes' in his eyes: his mother had grown increasingly anxious and childish, especially since his father's accident. (Father had survived a multiple crash on his way to work, but had been crushed in the wreckage for hours. After that he was a 'nervous jelly' and never really recovered.) Neil's own life had been pretty arid – he had dedicated himself to getting a degree, a job, and leaving home, and his feelings were generally subdued – but he was enthusiastic and hopeful about his future, despite feeling acutely the irony that his new job was in the transport industry, the source of his father's decline.

The one-sidedness of Neil's life pointed, no doubt, to some quite serious underlying problem, but he had set and achieved his own goals against heavy odds, and on the whole seemed emotionally robust and resilient, despite his extreme behaviour. Given that, and the very limited time available, it seemed entirely appropriate merely to help him understand his suicidal impulses in terms of his anxieties about the effects his success would have on him and his parents: could he get on and leave behind his damaged parents, or did he too have to be crushed and jelly-like? This was a temporary hitch in a reasonably well-managed life.

Mandy's story is a different one:

She was a very depressed girl who spent hours weeping on her own or in the middle of her family. When she had exhausted herself with tears, she was bright and cheerful, studied diligently, and helped with the household necessities. She had left home twice to escape awful arguments with her mother, who had two lines of response to her distress: either she would feel better when her exams were over, or she nothing to complain about because her (mother's) life had been far worse to bear. Mother had indeed been hospitalized several times, once immediately after Mandy's birth, when she had been farmed out to friends and relatives. The parents divorced soon after that, father disappeared from the scene, and mother was again in no state to look after her properly. They had no settled home until mother remarried some ten years later. Mandy felt that she belonged nowhere and with no one. She bitterly resented having to look after herself and indeed had no internal image of a good mother to help her do that. Her schooling was her one area of success, and she could think of herself only as a brain or as sick. Although she was determined to get to Oxbridge, the future seemed entirely pointless and meaningless to her. Relationships were futile and disappointing.

Mandy wasn't attempting to manage and redeploy her resources or to redefine herself: she was seeking an identity that she had never had. Although she appeared to be an aggressively intelligent young woman, whom no one would suspect had problems, she was hiding within her a stunted baby who would no longer submit to neglect and was making a last-ditch bid for serious and capable attention, before the intellectual façade cemented over once and for all.

Winnicott (1972) has developed the concept of the 'false self': the outwardly coping and managing (sometimes extremely successfully) façade that shelters the true self, which is too frightened and vulnerable to venture past the crenellations of the façade. The life of such a person is a perpetual lie, and like all lies, is brittle and precarious; but it is a lie that at least permits the truth to survive if not to thrive. The falseness tends to be exposed at points of major change when personal identity has to be examined and adjusted. Consequently, this kind of person turns up for help towards the end of adolescence, in his late twenties when major career and personal questionings occur, or in that movable crisis of mid-life when intimations of mortality arouse now-or-never anxieties. An overwhelming sense of futility is the hallmark of these people: nothing seems worth while, effort seems pointless, no experience touches them in an engaging way, relationships feel empty, hopes are delusions, and even satisfactions and triumphs soon turn to nought. Usually they can express this meaninglessness in very direct and desolate ways.

> Nancy has just been promoted and seemed set for a highly satis-factory career which used her remarkable quiet orderliness and effic-iency. She, however, became severely depressed. One lunchtime she was wandering along the river and 'saw' her own face smiling at her from the other bank. She returned to her office and wreaked havoc, throwing everything into a heap in the middle of the room. Sometime later she was discovered crouching and crying silently in a corner. She refused to speak - indeed probably couldn't. Denuded of her pictures and plants, her office seemed dingy and oppressive. Suddenly a bird sang outside, and Nancy, looking out the window, but pointing at herself, wailed 'What's a beautiful bird like you doing

in a dump like this?' She was drawing attention to her fragile, creative self which was in danger of being smothered for ever by her apparent success.

THE FOUNDATIONS OF THE SELF

Because the question of personal identity is so crucial for young people, it is essential for the counsellor to be able to distinguish between those who are having to find themselves for the first time and those who are merely having to reshape themselves, that is, between those who have never felt firmly grounded in their own experience and can't say 'I am' with any conviction, and those who know who they are despite confusion, anxiety and change. This means returning to the 'global' phase of development to look more closely at ego formation.

Before entering again into the infant's mind and feelings, however, perhaps it is timely to note a linguistic muddle which can lead to a theoretical muddle and to pursue an extended analogy which draws together the ideas about levels of disturbance. The concept of 'ego' tends to be used indiscriminately, when at least two definitions should be kept clearly separate (leaving aside the popular use, as in 'ego-trip' and 'ego-maniac', which generally implies conceit and selfishness). One is the Freudian Ego, part of his id-ego-superego triumvirate. This is the part of the individual which negotiates between the clamourous impulses of the id and the moralizing censorship of the superego and removes conflicts through the psychological acrobatics which are the defences. It also monitors and mediates the relationship between the self and the environment, evaluating the effectiveness of its own defensive manoeuvres and modifying them as necessary. As such it is a very active function and might be more aptly thought of as a verb than a noun. We all need and live on these ego defences; the term need not be perjorative. The other ego is a broader concept which refers to the personal self, an organized identity, our unique being, within which the activities of the Ego can go on. It is the 'I am' based on feeling continuous and worth while. There are obvious similarities between the two concepts, because they both arise out of attempts to adapt to the environment and to become viable within it, but the self is about holding, and the Ego is about holding in: the difference between the skin and a corset, perhaps.

Now for the simple metaphor of a house. The solid and well-entrenched foundation upon which the house is built can be seen as the equivalent of the self as an organized, continuous and worthwhile (purposeful and indispensable) entity. It defines the beginning of the house and separates it from the earth upon which it is built. It provides protection from the natural forces of the ground and is the framework for the rest of the building. Without it the house cannot stand as an integrated structure. However, even with a good foundation, things can go wrong with the construction of the house: faulty materials or faulty craftsmanship leave flaws which require repairs and patching-up. The building and the patching-up are like the work of the protecting and defending ego. No house is perfect, but the more carefully and lovingly it is originally built, the fewer repairs it will need. In terms of levels of disturbance, the patchings-up represent the neurotic disorders and the seriousness is equivalent to how fundamental to the basic structure the repairs are. An inadequate foundation results in psychosis. Any house-owner will be able to extend this metaphor from personal experience, but here are some random examples. High-rise buildings are built with carefully constructed flexibility; they have to sway with the wind and contract and expand with heat. Built too loosely or too rigidly, they collapse. Similarly, in hurricane conditions, a house which is completely barricaded against the wind can be blown over, while an insufficiently secured house gets messed up inside. This is what is meant by defences being necessary to protect structure and content – but if they are too rigid they defeat the whole purpose. In human terms, we have to be available and responsive to enough of the environment, but we have to protect ourselves from destructive over-stimulation. Moving down to the foundation: the hastily thrown up dwellings of refugee camps are apparently complete houses, located on a plot of ground, but the foundations are not firmly embedded. The inhabitants live in them because of some traumatic upheaval experienced in a hostile environment. The houses are meant to be temporary dwellings only, but they often become permanent and, over time, the structures are developed and decorated according to the needs and personalities of the occupants. But the refugees never gain a sense of real security and belonging there; they continue to feel displaced from their homes and lives. Although to all appearances they carry on the ordinary business of living, they are never free from anxiety and uncertainty, can never settle because they anticipate another traumatic move or hope to return home to begin again: their lives are deprived of continuity. This is the fate of the false self who appears to live ordinarily but never feels he lives meaningfully because he has not grown up from his true foundations.

How, then, does the human baby lay the foundations of his self, and what happens to knock him askew, causing him to hide within a falsely developing structure? Most of what follows is based on the work of Winnicott (1972) and Guntrip (1968).

Winnicott states that there is no baby without a mother, which confronts us immediately with the paradox that the self requires a relationship in order to form and develop despite the fact that initially it (the self) is not organized. Something very clearly exists from the outset, but perhaps it is best described as an unintegrated and undifferentiated conglomeration of movements and sensations which have neither names nor meanings to the baby who is creating and experiencing them. He is totally and catastrophically dependent on his mother for survival – dependent on her capacity to identify with his internal state, to make sense of and respond appropriately to his tensions. In order for this to happen, both mother and baby maintain the illusion that the pre-natal state still exists. She continues to make space for him within her personal boundary and meets his biological needs without clear signals from him: she has to be omnipotent and omniscient. The boundary is also, of course, his boundary, and she marshalls it carefully, letting inside whatever they need for nourishment and stimulation and keeping out whatever is noxious. To a large extent the father helps with this. By doing all this she keeps her baby away from the brink of the 'unthinkable anxieties' of annihilation and engulfment, from being overwhelmed by fear. This happens both physically and psychologically, and the two reinforce each other. Not only does she create a containing state of mind where her baby's needs become her needs, but she parallels this physically by holding him. Clearly she is *doing* something for him, but more crucially she is *being* something for him: she is being the baby's self until he can be it for himself. It is because of this that Winnicott says a baby's ego is as good as his mother's ego-support.

While the mother is so omnipotent, so is the baby. By intuitively matching her responses to his needs as exactly as possible, she creates the illusion for the baby that there is an external reality which corresponds precisely to what he would create as ideal for himself. The baby imagines that he *has* created it and that the world *is* him. This phase is absolutely critical for the baby because it gives him the sense of being in control of himself and the world, of being an initiator in his environment. However, this phase has to end. Just as mother and baby needed the physical separation of birth, they now need psychological separation for development to continue. Both have to relinquish the illusion of management by magical omnipotence for management according to reality. The mother's task is now to fail in her perfect adaptation – she strives for fallibility, but gradually, according to her baby's capacity to cope with her 'failure'. She gives him time and space to signal his needs and delays her responses and may even refuse to gratify him. This happens quite naturally as she moves out of her total preoccupation with him and responds to the demands and invitations of the rest of the environment. The baby can learn the meaning of his internal sensations because his mother responds specifically to specific signals from him, and through her fallibility he begins to recognize and discriminate between internal and external reality. The introduction of interrelatedness permits the baby to exist in his own right as separate, and it establishes the reality of himself and others as beings capable of love and hate, of being loved and hated. The necessary frustration disillusions him about his omnipotence – he doesn't after all possess and control all the resources he needs – and if he hasn't to wait too long, he gains a realistic sense of his power and helplessness in relation to others.

The process of sorting out what is him and what is not-him, where he has control and where he doesn't, goes on for years; the child uses both people and objects (particularly toys) to help him. It is through this early, gentle process of disillusionment, however, that he gains a fundamental sense of himself as a continuous and worthwhile person. He learns to rely on the fact that there will be gaps in his well-being, but that these are temporary, manageable and not totally disruptive. He knows that someone cares enough for and about him to provide that 'good-enough' experience. From this he emerges intact as a whole, initiating, firmly based and functioning self.

But what happens when these conditions don't prevail, when the infant hasn't been at once stimulated and protected and allowed to experience just as much of the real world as he could manage? Because the baby cannot survive on his own and has no experience with which to order his internal sensations, if left too much on his own he really is in danger of dying, biologically or psychologically. Psychological 'death' is the result of consistently adverse conditions and the baby's response to them. Many of us will know the anxiety and helplessness of being with a suffering baby whose crying changes from distress to panic if his pain cannot be eased. For the baby the unbearable pain seems endless and only stops when he is emotionally and physically exhausted. His internal terror is accompanied by fear of the hostile world which caused and failed to alleviate his pain. The onslaught from inside and outside threatens to annihilate him – his feelings become a threat to existence rather than a part of his existence – and the self protects itself by withdrawing into hiding behind defensive barriers. Guntrip puts this nicely in his formulation that the child was badly disturbed, but was too weak to alter his environment, so he altered himself to no longer feel weak and frightened or sought to know that he did not feel that way. The self is now no longer unified but is split into the weak and frightened part which, because it is in hiding, does not actually have a chance to grow, and the defensive part which continues to function in the world either aggressively or compliantly. Continuity has been disrupted, and the individual lives entirely on his defences, able only to react to real or anticipated impingements: the world out there always has the upper hand, and the best he can do is cope with whatever comes his way. Initiative is lost completely. This and the effort to appease the world so that it will not be aggressive or hostile is what is meant by compliance. Existence is reduced to a continual effort – rather like walking in an exposed area in strong gusts of wind, where he is constantly putting a shoulder into the wind in order not to be stopped or blown backwards; a very expensive way to live.

Being left alone with anxiety can be experienced either as the absence of a presence or as the presence of an absence. The first occurs when, for some reason, the person who is ordinarily there is gone, and the anticipated protection and holding is missing. This was Mark's experience. For the child, of course, the temporary absence feels eternal, since he has no concept of time or of living through time. The other, the presence of an absence, happens when the caring person is physically there, but psychologically not there for the child. The mother may be so depressed or preoccupied with her internal state or external problems that she has no time and energy left to care for her child. She excludes him from her personal boundary and is actually unavailable to him and ignores his signals to her. This leaves the infant feeling quite unreal, as well as abandoned to his anxieties. He lacks the sense of continuity which arises out of being in relationship, cannot take his being for granted, and instead has to resort to activity and concentration on his bodily states in order to feel real at all.

Development can also go awry when the mother is, in a sense, too good and ends up intruding into the child's space. She is too identified with the baby, needs to keep him undifferentiated from her, and doesn't allow him to exist in his own right. These mothers cannot or will not give up the magical management for a reality based relationship. In doing so, of course, she deprives her baby of the chance to gain control of himself and his world. The baby then has a choice of regression to merged dependence (as did Brendan) or of rejecting any care offered to him in a spurious attempt at separation.

Mandy had two dreams which reflect her early experience. In the first, she is running across a bridge and falls into the river. She can't swim but thrashes to a floating structure. This is slippery and unstable, so she can't get her balance and can't grip it. People are standing on it, including her mother, but no one moves to help her. She wakes up terrified and exhausted. In the second she is held as a hostage in an underground hide-out. There are other hostages, including her father, but they are released and go away. She knows she is going to be killed. Again she wakes terrified and exhausted. Both dreams clearly convey how she felt at the mercy of a hostile world and abandoned by her parents, who had their own problems, to her overwhelming terror: her fate was annihilation.

THE QUALITIES OF THE FALSE SELF

The 'personality' of the false self can, of course, develop in a variety of ways in different people, but they are almost always elusive and private individuals, who feel threatened by close relationships. They have an aggressive, often arrogant, coping style which automatically keeps people at bay, certainly forestalls sympathy, and may even elicit admiration for cool management of difficult situations. They tend to keep impossibly busy and are often high-achievers, although their achievements mean nothing to them. Doing things reassures them that they are alive, and they seek their value in the products of their doing. Unfortunately they do not find it because they unconsciously recognize that any success cannot be linked up with their true self which is so concealed. To use Guntrip's schema again: 'doing', in order to be personally significant and satisfying, must arise spontaneously out of a fundamental sense of being; or, to quote Mark: 'I am only as good as my last project.' With the beginning of each new project he has to start from square-one again. Only the failures are remembered, and adverse criticism is devastating.

This readiness to feel ashamed is also characteristic of the false self. Shame, the response to failure to achieve a self-set (and often secret) standard of behaviour, needs to be differentiated from guilt, which is evoked by the transgression of a rule. In unimpeded development, the child who reaches the 'sometimes' phase has a realistic evaluation of himself, and he can tolerate his fallibility. He retains an ego-ideal as a goal, but he expects to fall short of it sometimes. He is an *ordinary* person, with the possibility of being *extra*-ordinary, but he is neither ideally perfect nor ideally imperfect. The false self hasn't reached this state, he is still in the 'either-or' phase with its lingering shades of omnipotence and where the ideally good and bad still populate his world. The façade is also, of course, a product of omnipotence because it contains a refusal to be weak and vulnerable, a refusal to be touched by people and events around him. For him the ideal self is a must, not a possibility. Behaviour and feelings which conflict with or fall short of the ideal are unacceptable because they threaten to devastate all that he clings to as valuable about him and because the failure to cope reactivates the original catastrophic anxieties.

Mark had been extremely, even prematurely, successful at many things, all of which had required tremendous personal effort. He wanted help because he no longer felt successful, but asking was a dreadful humiliation, equivalent to acknowledging the weak, vulnerable - and despised - baby inside. Mark experienced any reference during the early stages of counselling to his baby self or to any less than perfect feeling as a wholesale attack on him and he responded with a ferocious assertion of all his achievements and 'glossy mags' life. By doing that, he preserved the only kind of continuity he knew, but it exposed his entirely defensive, and shame-ridden, existence. A dream expressed the unhappy relationship between the true and false self: he, as he now is, comes up some stairs and meets a small boy and a man. He asks the man where the wife and mother is, and the small boy turns on him angrily, ordering him out. Mark recognized the small boy as himself – the little one who simultaneously wants to be found and to stay hidden.

Awareness of the process of the formation of the unified self, and the ways in which it can be split, is important for counsellors working with young people because they are inevitably struggling to establish their identity, either as part of the normal transition to adulthood or fundamentally for the first time. The already firmly grounded ones still have to cope with sometimes alarming internal turmoil caused by new experiences in a larger world, so they need protection from being assaulted by more than they can handle. They need to learn to tolerate frustration and disillusionment when the world is less than they hoped and they can do less than they imagined. They are trying to find ways of taking realistic initiatives and having reasonable control in their lives. They need to know who they are, so what they do expresses that. Obviously the role that parents play in this stage of development, as described earlier, is exactly parallel to the function of the 'good-enough' mother who gradually yields absolute responsibility, and frustrates and disillusions her child at his pace. A counsellor may well be doing the same thing; but she may also sometimes have to provide it 'from the beginning' for those who are trying to find themselves for the first time and who are less concerned about the anxieties around growing up than about trust and simple survival. She needs to know that this is what is necessary and not to treat the 'wrong' person by concentrating on the ups and down of the façade.

THE HEALTHY PERSONALITY

These first chapters have been mostly about ways in which emotional development can go wrong. Emotional disturbance is clearly relative in so far as each individual has his own level of tolerance for tension and conflict. By the same token, 'normality' is also relative, but perhaps it is appropriate to end this section with an attempt to decribe that elusive 'normal' character. He is, first of all, more or less effortlessly adaptable and flexible. He lives in the real world of the present, not the past or the future. His past is in its proper place - his earlier experiences are memories, not currently active influences - and his future is anticipated with curiosity, not forestalled by efforts to control it. Because he can say 'I' with conviction, he is willing to subject himself to reasonable experience and can take risks with it both by using opportunities given to him and making opportunities for himself. He has some clarity about what he needs and wants - indeed has sorted out the significant difference between them - and knows whence it is appropriate to expect satisfaction. As well as being able to extend himself, he has adequate and effective means of protecting himself against the unnecessarily unpleasant and anxious-making. Finally, he can accept responsibility for himself and for others and is his own agent: he initiates and responds instead of being driven by and reacting to forces inside and outside himself.

Does such a person exist?

4 ‖ The counselling relationship

The therapeutic work of counselling might be to help the client attain a state of health and well-being, but few counselling encounters are ever so overtly ambitious. Indeed, the client who opened her first session with the statement 'I want to be made normal' had, as it turned out, very limited aims for herself. However extensive the hopes and aims of the client, and however specific the problem and the goal, the route to that end involves helping the client make sense of himself, his feelings and his experience so that he may regain possession of himself and live effectively in his world. Perhaps this happens through gaining a different perspective of himself and his life, perhaps through transforming feelings and experiences into shapes that are more useful and meaningful than they had been before, but it never happens through destroying what already is: like matter, feelings and experiences cannot be destroyed but they can be changed into something as apparently different as steam is from ice. These central chapters attempt to describe what happens when client and counsellor actually meet together to pursue those aims along those routes. Ostensibly they need to talk about the client and his world – but it is a special kind of talking, in a particular kind of relationship, with a distinctive milieu. Even so, as the various aspects of these moods, relationships and languages are unfolded, counselling reveals itself to be a rather protean creature.

CREATING THERAPEUTIC SPACE

Descriptions of counselling are usually couched in verbs, in terms of doing, of implementing technical mechanisms. Doing is, of course, crucial to the work, but what is done and what happens are effective because they take place within the counselling relationship and within a therapeutic atmosphere. Counsellors don't have a monopoly on listening and communicating in a helpful way; but in establishing the relationship and acknowledging that the process of counselling is going on, they do create something different from an ordinary friendship or conversation. They provide a space free from everyday assumptions and demands, where façades can be relaxed, and they provide the presence of another who absorbs, contains and gives meaning to what happens in that space. The importance of the relationship was under-lined by a supervisor who told a trainee who was worrying about getting interpretations right, 'What you actually say doesn't matter nearly so much as the fact that you are there every time.' Another supervisor told his new trainee that they would, quite rightly, spend the first half of their time establishing the relationship and the last half ending it – there is no person for whom the feelings and difficulties around beginning, sustaining and ending a relationship are irrelevant. Using the relationship as a way of 'doing' counselling is one of the aspects of the work discussed extensively later, but at this point what matters is the fact of the relationship itself, and the implications of that for the client.

Françoise Dolto (1974) uses the concept of the counsellor or therapist being a witness to all that is said and done in the therapeutic encounter. She uses it in the restricted sense of simply giving evidence of the *existence* of the client and his activity. No matter what it is, it is real; it exists because it has been observed by another who regards it as real and meaningful. This in itself may be therapeutic, especially for clients who are accustomed to having themselves or their words, feelings and actions dismissed, ignored, mocked or otherwise rendered meaningless, but it is perhaps the relatedness that is critical for the client. Not only has his activity been made real, but it has also been given a place and a meaning in the relationship between himself and the counsellor, and so it no longer exists as an isolated and insignificant episode in his experience. People do, as we have already seen, seek for and find their self and their significance in a relationship with another. Without a sense of belonging, nothing makes any real sense; with a sense of belonging, what happens is both concretely and symbolically signi-ficant. In this way, the counselling situation resembles the primary maternal relationship, described by Winnicott, in which the mother *is* something for the infant more than she *does* things for him. Without actually establishing a regressed mother-infant relationship, a counsellor can meet the fundamental needs for that relatedness and for that space within which personal exploration and discovery can go on without interference from 'grown-up' demands and consequences.

This space, this environment facilitating growth and personal discovery, is created and preserved by the counsellor's ability to keep the external, everyday world at bay but not denied; to maintain a helpful distance between herself and the client; and to keep the internal and external worlds in perspective. At the very practical level, she protects the sessions against intrusions from other people and other demands by fixing the time and place as an inviolate framework, and in doing so relieves the client of such reality responsibilities. By assuming these ego functions in connection with the external world on behalf of her client, she implicitly sanctions his giving up, for the time being, the coping mechanisms which ensure his orderly functioning in the world of chronological time and geographical space. More than that, she indicates that it doesn't matter that it is actually 3 o'clock on Tuesday afternoon in this room: for the duration of the session psychological time and space take over, and the client is free to move around in his subjective world as he will without the constraints of the objective world. It is not, however, an invitation to abdicate responsibility for what happens in the session. Such protection is also necessary for the counsellor as well, since she has to be free from distraction in order to immerse herself in the client's subjective world and be completely available to him. (In so far as her own internal world permits, of course: she cannot shut out her urgent personal preoccupations by putting an 'engaged' sign on her mind.)

MAINTAINING BOUNDARIES

Being completely available for the client means putting emotional, intellectual, perceptual and intuitive capabilities at his service, using them to understand what it feels like to be him in his world, to identify with him and his dynamic situation, while yet remaining firmly outside his world. Attention is free-floating but disciplined, ready to pick up any subtle, unarticulated or unconscious message from the client, ready to elaborate it experimentally with associations and to test it against assumptions in order to feel and understand the communications. It requires emotional effort to become so immersed in another person's system and even more effort to remain involved but detached: it requires the apparently contradictory actions of letting go of yourself

and remembering who you are. It is crucial for the client that the counsellor doesn't lose her personal boundaries and get lost in his world; she
must remain quite distinct and separate from him, whole and intact
within herself. Muddled or missing personal boundaries are
frightening.

In a first interview Danny struggled inarticulately against shame and
confusion to explain why he had come. Having made several
attempts to describe a series of problems, without really completing
any of them, he began to talk about how he makes copious notes
about things and studies them before going to a dinner party to make
sure he will have something to say. The counsellor, having registered
several concrete and symbolic references to food and hunger and feeling herself rather emotionally hungry for a complete description/
meal, commented that it sounded like needing a big meal as a safeguard against going hungry. Danny was both excited and frightened
by the comment. It helped him to cut through several peripheral
worries to arrive at his central and most shameful feeling of being
emotionally starved following the break-up of a relationship, which
in turn set off memories of being farmed out, when his brother was
born, to an emotionally cold lady who made unforgettably inedible
scrambled eggs every day for tea; but he felt psychologically invaded,
as if his mind had been read magically. The counsellor could demonstrate to him that he was leading her to this event through the
references he had already made, and through making her feel
frustrated and unfed by his manner of talking about himself: they
were still quite separate, not symbolically merged, but they could
communicate emotionally as well as literally and that would help in
the work together.

The 'just right' balance of being emotionally within the client's
dynamic system and intellectually monitoring that involvement is the
essence of the therapeutic stance of maintaining a helpful distance from
the client. For it to happen the counsellor must be 'together', at peace
with herself and very secure about her own boundaries. Consequently
she can be neither too obtrusive nor too unobtrusive in the relationship. If a counsellor is too anxious, too personally turbulent, too tired, if
her internal world too closely matches her client's, or if she emotion-

ally rejects her client's messages, then that helpful distance is lost and communication becomes either an invasion or a dead end.

Ted had bought a second-hand desk and talked urgently about the junk he had found in a drawer – bits of torn-up paper, odds and ends that might not belong in a desk, broken things all jumbled up. The counsellor thought that he was telling her that he felt chaotic and broken up inside. There was no other immediate evidence for this, but he had had badly disturbed episodes before, so she was uncertain. Both rather hoped these episodes were a thing of the past, and at that particular point in time the counsellor was herself feeling 'in a mess' and didn't feel she could cope with his mess, even if she could work out whose mess it was. She sat and debated whether she was sure enough to say anything and was ultimately paralysed with uncertainty. After he left, she was quite positive that that was his message, and a letter from him confirmed it: he wrote that he was feeling crazy again, but he hadn't been able to tell her. He did and didn't want her to know. His dilemma had totally invaded the counsellor and met her dilemma of knowing and not wanting to know.

The delicate and moving balance between being within and without the client's dynamic system – of being neither too close nor too remote – is nicely conveyed in Kahn's (1974) statement: You have to suffer along with the patient, but not suffer like the patient.

In a second example, the counsellor's anxiety completely shut out her client's communications and led to a break in the relationship; she couldn't even suffer along with the client.

Clare had been a very demanding client from the beginning. She had apparently already defeated one therapist who was said to have become 'over-involved' with her, and she was making insidious inroads into her counsellor's private life. She was asking for help with her homosexual feelings and had from the start related to her female counsellor in a sexually seductive way. Forewarned by knowledge of the previous relationship and somewhat angered by the overt seductions, the counsellor had steadfastly refused to be inveigled into a personal relationship. In the session when she told Clare that their next meeting would have to be cancelled, Clare barraged her with a long and detailed account of how her best and idealized friend had snubbed her. Her bewildered indignation and dramatic despair over the sexual rejection made the counsellor feel so irritated that she managed to 'forget' about the cancelled session and its meaning for this very dependent girl. It wasn't until Clare failed to come for the next scheduled meeting that she realized how impervious she had been to Clare's real need for acceptance contained in her protest but hidden beneath the sexual flourishes.

Keeping personal boundaries intact and maintaining the helpful distance automatically ensure that the autonomy and individuality of the client are respected. The counsellor can allow the client to explore and discover his own world and experience his own feelings rather as contained parents can permit a child to explore without crowding his space with warnings and encouragements based on their own experience and anxieties. Although there are some 'universalities' about people, each has his own idiosyncratic experience of those commonalities. The counsellor might have some general assumptions, but she cannot presume about specific details, which can be discovered only by staying in close emotional contact with the interaction between the two as it proceeds. It is likely, perhaps, that the racket of a pneumatic drill in the street outside will annoy everyone, but not everyone will deal with it in the same way. Some clients will be overtly angry about the interference, others will sit in defeated silence, but not many will mentally sing a Bach concerto as a more pleasing background while carrying on as if nothing were happening outside, as did one very musical girl who had extraordinary powers of concentration. Misunderstanding a client's subjective experience is forgivable, but failing to try to understand his uniqueness by applying assumptions or textbook explanations glibly is not. Observing a client in glances over the top of an open textbook turns him into a case to be studied, not a person to understand for his own sake. The distance is too great, the exercise too impersonal; it is a personal affront, and the lack of human respect invites withdrawal of trust which is essential for the therapeutic work to go on at all.

Clients, in their need for certainty and a rapid resolution to their pain, sometimes want their counsellor to rush in with premature or magical explanations. They may even expect it as part of her professional experience and her 'duty' - 'You *must* know - you've seen

hundreds of people and must have come across my problem before.'
Indeed she may, but that misses the inescapable point that each individual lives his own life (and problems) in his own way. Her response to
that appeal is that she might have seen many people, but she has never
worked with *this* particular individual before. Even presuming that the
counsellor does know the right explanation and can give it to her client,
that puts him in the position of a passenger being taken somewhere by
someone who already knows the route. He is much less likely to know
how to get there again than is the person who had to work out the
route for himself. Allowing (or making) him arrive at and own his
knowledge of himself so he can use it subsequently is an antidote to
dependence. Futhermore, and more important, counselling is not
primarily an intellectual exercise: the emotional engagement is the
therapeutic element. Insight, on its own, is not enough.

HOLDING THE PERSPECTIVE

Although it is important to stick closely to the interaction and to attend
to the minute nuances of details, it is equally important for the counsellor to stand well back in order to encompass the whole of the client.
By doing this, she may well give him a new perspective on himself.
Usually clients come with some quite specific complaint: they present a
symptom or a problem which they want removed or cured; many will
focus on it as the sole topic of discussion. Particularly those who feel
assailed by a symptom as if it were an alien body ('this panic just comes
over me out of the blue') or those who have so identified themselves
with the problem that it has taken them over ('I am a claustrophobic')
will return time and again to report on the state of the problem: it has
disappeared altogether for a couple of days, has a new twist, is worse,
and so on. They know it intimately, all its nuances and subtleties, all
their reactions to it, as if the symptom itself has a status of an individual
being with a flourishing personality. However, despite being able to say
so much about it, the talking aggrandizes the symptom and tends to
entrench rather than shift it. The counsellor doesn't react in this way
to the problem: she doesn't overvalue it and doesn't mistake the
problem for the person. Instead she sees the person as a dynamically
functioning system. The symptom is the visible malfunction in the
system and probably reflects some invisible malfunction which in turn

affects how the system is working as a whole. She tries to find its place in his total psychological make-up and through a wide exploration of his current and historical life follows and links its causes and reverberations. Consequently a lot of time can go by without the original problem being mentioned. Clients will mostly accept this as legitimate counselling activity, but not always.

Deborah was referred for counselling because her hands shook whenever she ate and drank in public, and she hated to be watched when she did anything using fine hand movements. Despite recognizing that the shaking only occurred in these specific situations, she believed the problem was neurological and only grudgingly complied with the referral for 'nerves'. However, she enjoyed chatting about herself, her parents and boyfriend, her work and hobbies – unless the subject of anger came up. Her counsellor felt there was strong unacknowledged anger and disappointment in the complaining and cynical undertones of her descriptions, but if she tried to explore this, Deborah would vehemently reassert her symptom: she'd point out it was still there and all this talk was useless. The repeated pattern of response convinced the counsellor that through her shaking hands Deborah was saying 'I'm itching to hit out at people who have let me down, but in our ultra-nice family, that is unthinkable and certainly can't be talked about.' Her refusal to accept the link between her body and her denied feelings ultimately brought the work to grief.

In so far as the symptom does contain a major internal conflict, it is easy to see how clients experience it as an enemy or as the focus for the whole self, and it is understandable that they get caught up in the grip of this view of themselves. It falls, therefore, to the counsellor to keep the wider perspective, to avoid colluding with such personal myopia, and to uphold the integrity of her client. Integrity is about wholeness, and the counsellor is there to help her client begin to mend himself by acknowledging his problem as part of himself – neither separate from, nor all of, him.

One specific therapeutic implication of holding the whole of the client in mind is recognizing the existential conflict over change within himself. She acknowledges and respects in him both his seeking and his hiding behaviour, both his healthy and his ill aspects. Paradoxically, the client has a right to his problem and his way of life, and no one has the right or authority to take it away from him or make it different. No one comes from counselling free of ambivalence: they want help, but they don't want to change because of all the anxieties associated with change.

> Julia, who had never allowed herself to have an even potentially sexual relationship, promised her counsellor that if she ever became interested in a man, she would give her a bouquet of flowers. Eventually that day did come, and she stormed into her session with a magnificent bunch of chrysanthemums which she flung down on the table muttering 'Thanks. Now I've got another whole lot of problems for us.'

Julia and her counsellor had managed to work on her anxieties about change co-operatively, so that her reluctance to face the consequences of that change could emerge directly, and even delightfully. The reluctance is usually less amenable, however. It is frustrating and confusing to work with someone who says he wants to change, but drags his feet, misses appointments, or overtly rejects whatever help is offered. In response to this, and in order not to bully the client or to ignore the resistance completely, counsellors do sometimes agonize over how to behave differently so the client will come and work. It is as if they have to change to spare the client the effort of changing. It seems to feel particularly dangerous to mention the negative side, the side that prefers things to stay as they are, but in ignoring it, the counsellor is herself being defensive. Perhaps the most tangible area where this happens is attendance. When a client is consistently late or misses planned meetings, every time with a plausible reason, it is difficult to remember that this is also a message about his ambivalence about therapy. Accepting the offered reason as simple and valid often results in the client's despairing over not being completely comprehended and his being burdened by guilt about his negative feelings which apparently must not be discussed.

All these attitudes to the client and the work create the therapeutic environment. The effort to balance the internal and the external world, to attend closely to detail but not at the expense of the larger wholeness of the person, and to engage emotionally and intellectually with his internal world while keeping both his and the counsellor's intact is tremendous but essential to the primary task of providing a secure and facilitating space, and respecting the client in his struggle to make sense of or change his personal world. Above all, perhaps, the counsellor takes her client seriously. He comes in a state of pain and conflict which cannot be easily eliminated, and the counselling work arouses its own pain and conflict. None of that can be taken lightly. She can laugh at the jokes and share the genuinely funny side of things, but on the whole, counselling is a serious, although not necessarily a solemn, business.

THE FACETS OF THE RELATIONSHIP

Within the therapeutic space the counsellor and client engage with each other in a number of different ways and at different levels. They work and play, have a real and a transference relationship, and build together a secure trust which allows emotional exploration. These activities alternate and merge, according to the needs of the client in his movement toward the resolution of his difficulties. In the relationship it is not always easy to separate them clearly, but here we can do so arbitrarily for the purpose of discussion.

Play

Having said that counselling is serious, it might seem contradictory to say that it is also playful. To the extent that the immediate demands and conventions of the everyday world are set aside for the duration, however, a counselling session becomes a magic circle in which the rules and terms of reference are different from those operating in reality. Anyone within the circle agrees to subscribe to those rules and terms and to engage seriously in the activity for the time being. The important thing, however, is that reality has been suspended or supplanted so the objective outcome doesn't matter. It doesn't matter because the relationship will survive almost anything. The absence of real, interpersonal catastrophe permits experimentation with feelings and ideas about the self and others which feel too dangerous for real life because of the consequences if it all goes wrong, although of course what happens in the magic circle is not completely dissociated from what happens outside it. Playing 'Monopoly' is very different from speculating in actual property, and the usually mean and miserly can, in the game, try out feeling spendthrift and aggressive. Losing the game may strain the relationship with the other players, but it won't result in appearing in court on charges of bankruptcy. Similarly pursuing a phantasy to its bitter or wonderful end in the counselling session, or discovering all the ins and outs of an unaccustomed feeling, may not make the phantasy come true nor automatically allow the feeling to be freely expressed elsewhere, but the work will affect other relationships later. Paradoxically, then, the space created for intense and effortful play is also a resting place where the client is protected from all the internal and external pressures of relating and coping.

Winnicott (1971) wrote eloquently about this sort of play relationship in his paper on 'transitional objects', discussing the interaction between a child and his 'cuddlies'. He describes how he uses – and needs to use – these things to discover what is 'me' and what is 'not-me': to find the boundaries of himself and establish his separateness from others. The essential features of such a toy or object are first, that it undeniably belongs to the child and is indeed practically inseparable from him, almost becoming an extension of him; and secondly, that it can never act on its own. No matter how loving or hating, brutal or caring, generous or selfish, concerned or callous the child is to it, it cannot act or retaliate; it won't laugh or cry, hug or bite back, demand more or run away, scold or praise. The child does imagine the feelings and behaviours that he hopes and fears will be aroused by his feelings and actions, and he animates his toy with them and incorporates them into his play. Nevertheless he remains mindful that the toy is really an inanimate object, so he learns that any feelings around are his, created by him, and that those feelings, in themselves, do not have objective consequences, even though behaviour based on feelings may. These transitional objects are chosen for their virtual indestructability: they can show scars of more vigorous activity, but can't be mutilated beyond recognition. The absence of serious consequences – they are both still there and more or less intact at the end of the episode – means that the child can enjoy all his feelings: he doesn't have to worry about how others will respond. Since he is usually in an active relationship with live, powerful and controlling people, the retreat to his teddy is indeed a psychological rest and a relief, a moment of freedom from objective anxiety.

The counselling relationship provides the client with a similar opportunity to relax from the world and to discover his own nature through playful experimentation. Because the counsellor keeps her own overt private feelings and responses outside the relationship, she becomes a kind of transitional object, the client's 'not-me'. He can, as it were, animate her with imagined responses, reactions, wishes and feelings about him, but he can also see that those are created by him out of his hope and anxieties. The need to manage only his own feelings, rather than the usual state of having to attend to both his own and others', brings its own kind of relief and even gives the sessions a rehearsal or familiarization element. He has time and space to get used to a new aspect of himself, to become accustomed to experiencing that sort of feeling, and to anticipate how others might respond before actually having to face others and their reactions. On the face of it, the capacity to intervene disqualifies the counsellor as a transitional object, but so long as the interventions are designed to help the client find and become acquainted with his feelings, her function is symbolically the same.

This sort of playing shades imperceptibly into exploration. In the process of play the client takes risks, tries new things and confirms old ones not only to find his personal limits but also to discover more about his environment and his relation to it. In so doing he expands his world. Exploration into the unknown is made possible, as we have seen, by a sense of security about one's self, the known environment, and the capacity to manage the unexpected. A toddler is the simplest analogy. He is intensely curious about his world and will make forays into it, but regardless of how fearless he may be, he still keeps within rapid returning distance of his secure base, be it his home or his mother. When he meets something bewildering, exciting or anxious-making, he rushes back for sharing and safety. The watchful mother lets this going and returning happen, interfering only to prevent real danger or to encourage her child to test out imagined danger against reality in a safe context: she may keep the child away from a temperamental Alsatian dog, but will hold her child and stroke the friendly sheep-dog which has frightened him.

In the counselling setting the same letting-be happens. Seldom does a counsellor have to act to prevent a client from real danger, but she does provide the safe environment within which the client can sort out reasonable and unreasonable fear, objective and subjective danger. The client brings to the session anxieties and risks encountered in his everyday world and leaves with the fruits of having shared and tested them with his counsellor; but he also encounters risks and anxieties within the session as he explores his internal world. Here the risks are connected with being confused, stuck or frightened at a point of personal discovery.

At such moments of fear it is tempting to be reassuring and to release the client from the task of confronting his anxiety, but that is not really helpful. Caring sometimes means being apparently tough. Being tough, however, is simply keeping in mind the purpose of the relationship. The kind, caring and protective aspects of providing space and security for play and exploration are readily accepted by client and counsellor as part of the relationship; the more aggressive aspect of maintaining a work relationship often seems less compatible with the notion of the client in distress. Making demands on the client to work may feel harsh at times, but letting opportunities for work slip by because it might be too painful is about as caring as sending a secretary home at lunchtime because she has too much work to do, knowing that tomorrow will bring yet more.

Work

Without in any way implying that counselling is just a job, it is work. It has a task, a purpose, sometimes even a contract, and the chances of its success depend on the ability of two people to work in a mutually inter-dependent fashion and to be clear about why they're there. As in any other working relationship, all sorts and levels of relating go on between client and counsellor simultaneously, all interacting, overlapping, merging and conflicting. Unlike most work, however, frequently the subject of the work is the relationship itself, since the evidence of the present interaction is the most effective data for tackling the primary task of helping the client deal with his difficulties.

The working partnership is founded on the participants' very ordinary feelings of liking each other simply as people. Such feelings are based on shared interests, compatible language, recognizing positive aspects of oneself in the other, and appreciating each other's personal style. It's certain that a crucial factor in therapeutic improvement is the counsellor's positive motivation toward her work and her client (she likes him, wants to help, and feels able to do so) and the client's complementary feeling that he likes, and can work with, the counsellor to get the best out of the relationship. The counselling relationship is just as prone as any other to instant and enduring inter-personal judgements, and it may rarely happen that something about one arouses antipathy in the other to such a degree that they cannot imagine working together. Usually the cause is quite specific, but if it collides with a patch of utter intolerance in the other, it is futile to behave as if they should be above such petty responses, and a particularly sensitive referral or transfer should be made. Negative feelings may, of course, arise in the course of the work and become grist for the counselling mill, but to start off with active dislike means forgoing the benign milieu and trust which are essential to get the difficult work off the ground at all. This basic liking also has to be genuine and free from panic or ulterior motives, not subject to mental acrobatics such as 'I like this person because I have to like her in order to get what she offers' or 'I like this person because if I don't he'll turn nasty on me.' Clients may well bring these elements of psychological survival to the relationship, but they are a different order of relating from simply feeling comfortable and compatible with each other. If they mask genuine and direct dislike, the relationship is fundamentally skewed from the start – just as it is when real liking is crowded out by hostility and anxiety about being in the relationship at all.

The basic requirement of liking each other underlines the fundamental fact that these are two ordinary people in the relationship. Clients often feel that they are no longer ordinary people and coming for counselling gives the stamp of veracity to feeling different, incomprehensible, silly, bad or ill. In so far as he regards himself as a lesser or extra-ordinary being he will not see the relationship as one of ordinary people. The counsellor also appears un-ordinary in the relationship in that her range of behaviour is quite limited, and the relationship itself is uneven by ordinary criteria. The client tells all, while the counsellor tells nothing, and there is an inherent contradiction between the great degree of intimacy and the 'clinical' limits placed on the relationship. However, most work relationships do have limits and are not all-providing and all-satisfying; they all have a particular language as the medium of the work, and some unevenness arises out of the roles designed to facilitate the work. The designated roles of the client and counsellor automatically invoke sets of actions and attributes, and evoke expectations about behaviour and attitudes.

Some of these are realistic and work-oriented, while others are phantasy-ridden, and may initially put counsellor and client at cross-purposes, as is the case, for instance, when the client expects to be helpless in the presence of the all-wise counsellor.

In reality, client and counsellor come together as two specialists, each having a particular expertise which needs to be linked to the other in order to be useful. The client is a specialist in his own life: no one knows better than he does how he came to be how he is in terms of historical and emotional data. Although he knows, he can't make use of that knowledge for reasons which also lie in his history and his feelings. The counsellor is a specialist in how and why people develop and in helping people bring out what they know. Unless the client brings his data, the counsellor cannot do her job; and unless the counsellor brings her ability to structure that data, the client cannot work with it. (It is said that Michelangelo said of his Pietà that he only released what already existed in the marble. The counsellor can likewise only bring out what is already in the person. But the skill is no trifling matter.) Both bring curiosity and hopefulness about the process and outcome of the work, and that, like the proverbial carrot, keeps them going over the rough patches.

The alliance

Along with their special expertise, each brings the intention and the motivation to co-operate in whatever will best help the client find out about himself and his world. It is tempting to say that the mature, healthy, rational part of the client engages with the counsellor to work on his immature, unhealthy and irrational part, and to some extent this is so: during the work the client holds on to a self-observing faculty which participates in and comments on dialogue with the counsellor. But such a division of the client into parts is inadequate and inaccurate as a description of the emotional rapport which permeates the relationship and forms the therapeutic alliance.

From the client's side, this alliance contains the wish to co-operate and accept help. It means accepting both the need for help and the responsibility of sharing the work involved in obtaining it. So it is more than the wish to get better or to be rid of the problem. Clients can express all these wishes, but merely stating them isn't sufficient. Agreement to receive counselling as a condition of probation, for instance, is not a therapeutic alliance when it is coerced and unrelated to the personal intentions of the probationer. It has to be internally generated, not externally imposed. The alliance is partly grounded in the client's ability to find some good in distress, and it may function like a safety-net: when it would appear that the relationship is going to flounder in a difficult phase, it is the underlying trust which sustains the work.

The alliance stems from basic trust in the self, the counsellor, and their relationship - trust that all three will survive anything and everything. It functions through the capacity of the client and counsellor to form an attachment, and to be dependent on each other. To refer to the phase of early development again: in the first months of life, a baby forms a strong emotional bond with one other person whom he discriminates as unique. Such a bond is necessary for biological survival and for psychological well-being: it enables him to get his bearings (feel placed and secure in a relationship) and to build up an internal image of himself through the way the other relates to him. This attachment is a source of stability and reliability in the midst of continuous change and growth. If deprived of this point of constancy, either through real separation or emotional unpredictability, then his sense of someone being there for him in moments of crisis is eroded and he is reluctant or unable to entrust himself in other relationships later on.

The episode of the relationship between the Little Prince and the fox in de St-Exupéry's *The Little Prince* (1945) describes the formation of an attachment more vividly and poignantly than any theoretical explanation ever can. The fox asks to be tamed, and he explains that this means that the Little Prince should mark him out as unique among all foxes, just as the Little Prince is unique among all men for the fox. Each then has a sense of responsibility for the other, anticipates and is glad to see the other, is reminded of him by other things (which gain meaning because they are reminders - as the golden wheat, which is useless for the fox, becomes important for him because it is the colour of the Little Prince's hair), and they are sad to lose each other. The pain of loss is, however, bearable because of all that has gone before.

Once the bond of attachment is formed between two people, all sorts of things can happen: care, concern, fear, hate, love, creation and destruction, independence and co-operation, trying out different ways of feeling and relating. Without that attachment, the two people are indifferent to each other, their feelings empty, and the interaction sterile. It is obvious that this kind of emotional investment is absolutely necessary in counselling when the medium of work is feelings and the meaning of events, people and objects in the client's world. Without the existence of this attachment, the work is virtually meaningless. Indeed, often the initial stages of the work are concerned with just this issue: the problems and anxieties concerned in becoming involved in this unique relationship. (Hence, of course, the significance of the two supervisors' comments mentioned earlier.)

The 'moral' of the relationship between the fox and the Little Prince, which stands out from his encounters with other people in the story who have some ulterior motive behind their interactions, is that such an attachment works and develops because it is free from panic and the need to satisfy some feeling which is incompatible with exploration and growth. Perhaps some examples of unhealthy dependence will help to illustrate how it prohibits growth and consequently does not contribute to the therapeutic alliance. There is the overtly and happily dependent person who imagines that he has at last found someone who will sort everything out if he sits quietly and hopefully long enough. The snag is that he doesn't really want things sorted out because he might then have to do something other than sit hopefully and helplessly, so his open mouth is, as it were, hermetically sealed. Being unready to work on his own behalf, and unrealistic in his expectations, he will probably become disillusioned and go off to try his luck elsewhere. Then there is the acquiescent person who surrenders all critical capacities to the counsellor, takes everything in, swallows it whole, and doesn't think about it. The work slides through these people, who behave like drain-pipes, without actually touching them meaningfully, although they may keep a memory store of 'useful comments' for which they express eternal gratitude.

On the other side are those who resist any kind of interpersonal dependence. They are stolidly mistrustful, terrified of dependency, but often recognizably dependent in a negative way: whatever goes wrong is blamed on someone or something else; they desperately need a person to blame. Finally come those who turn themselves inside out by saying that because they have to trust the counsellor, they will - but don't. Unless all these anxieties and conflicts around dependence and attachment are pursued at the outset and throughout the work, it can happen that all the time is wasted: instead of being genuinely allied in the therapeutic work, the client has been doing mental gymnastics which have distorted the meaning of the counselling relationship.

Obviously, the counsellor also has to develop and maintain the therapeutic alliance from her side. She has to keep her eye on the task in hand and not transform the relationship in order to satisfy something within herself which is incompatible with the development of the relationship and the client's personal growth. Meeks (1971) has vividly described the 'Unholy Alliances' which can tempt the counsellor. Adolescents issue particularly enticing invitations in these directions, sometimes all at once, as did one young man in his opening statement about himself. He announced that he had come for counselling because he was an 'acid casualty'. He expounded at length on all the good reasons for taking drugs, including the aspects of drug-induced personal insight and the excitement of illicit activity, followed by horrific examples of things that had happened to him on 'bad trips'. He wanted to get himself back together again, but he really didn't see the point because society is violent, exploitative and psychotic. For the counsellor it would be easy to get caught up in, and fascinated by, all the excitement in an alliance with the man's impulses; or to ally with the superego and come down with righteous indignation on the side of the law which is meant to protect people from bad trips; or rather than get to grips with the problems of his violence, exploitation, and perhaps psychosis, it could be diverting to engage in a philosophical conversation about the state of contemporary society in an alliance with his defences to postpone the evil moment of facing personal pain. None of these would have been very helpful to the client, but they might have temporarily satisfied the counsellor's needs.

A sturdy therapeutic alliance preserves the relationship from becoming either too social or too impersonal. Particularly as they develop positive feelings toward the counsellor and the work, clients may push for a more social relationship, wanting to meet in less formal circumstances or wanting a mutual exchange of personal feelings. Without denying any reality-based mutual liking, and without callously reminding the client that he is a client, the counsellor needs to clarify that social involvement would put an end to the counselling relationship, putting friendship in its place: the very necessary distance would be destroyed. Mutual exchange is outside the task of the work. In any case, the wish to alter the relationship is likely to be an expression of the current dynamic within the work. The timing of the wish to change is usually significant, reflecting anxiety or frustration: anxiety about the insights already, or about to be, gained; and frustration over not getting enough from the counsellor, so the client wants more, or a different sort of, care and attention. Such moments of anxiety are critical in the work, and the client needs help to stay with them. The frustration is equally therapeutic: if the counsellor is all- and perfectly providing, the client loses the opportunity to learn how to manage his frustration and has no incentive to seek satisfaction from others around him. (In practice, if it does happen that the two meet accidentally, the client is often flustered and retreats, or continues to relate as if counselling were still going on. When it comes to the crunch, they prefer not to know about the reality of the counsellor because they still need her as counsellor, not as someone to take account of socially.)

While some urge a less formal relationship, others go to the opposite extreme and refuse to acknowledge the counsellor's realness and the existence of a relationship at all. Transforming her into a cardboard dummy, or a disembodied ear and mouth, they hope to escape any of the positive and negative feelings that might arise about her and the work. Such a degree of detachment or denial is unrealistic and has to be understood as a defensive posture. It's the client's equivalent of the counsellor regarding him as a textbook example, stripped of any individuality and wholeness. Clients may need to preserve the idea of the counsellor as being without feelings or requirements, otherwise it is difficult to attack and demand and remain free from guilt. Unless they can let the counsellor be a real person, however, they never have the chance to find out if they really need to feel so guilty about their needs. If the counsellor acquiesces in this two-dimensional, impersonal image she has surrendered a major part of her therapeutic potential for the client.

Mark grumbled and complained that no one ever noticed how he was feeling. The counsellor had been unwell and distracted in the previous session, and in response to his complaints she commented on that last meeting, suggesting that he was irritated with her lack of attention then. He, of course, hadn't noticed how she was feeling and rather ungraciously and petulantly retorted that her problems were no business of his and he hoped she was better – meaning that she wasn't allowed to have her difficulties and 'off' days but should be in a perfect state for him. This incident confirmed her own growing feeling of being treated like an automatic coffee-machine, and she used it to confront him with his difficulty in relating to another whole person and his failure to notice other people's feelings. Consequently he was forever blundering and offending others, always bewildered when people were irritated by his selfishness, always causing people to ignore him and avoid his feelings.

Another example, picking out three incidents in a very long relationship with a seriously disturbed young man, demonstrates the sustaining power of an excellent therapeutic alliance.

A few weeks into the work, after a session spent in almost total silence, the counsellor received a letter from Ted in which he described his violent phantasies and then launched an attack on her for intending to change him into something he didn't want to be. It concluded with the statement that having written this he could no longer bear to come and face her. She wrote back asking him to come for one more session, without prejudice to the future. He came and they could discuss the 'fact' that despite the horrendous phantasies, she could still bear to know him and didn't hate him because there was far more to him than that – witnessed by his writing the letter in the first place.

Nearly two years later – time punctuated by some hospitalizations for his own protection, some very confused periods, more violence, but obviously some substantial work as well – during a difficult and painful phase of work on his anger over separations, Ted appeared in a mood of deadly calm and stood over the counsellor with a knife poised on his arm, barraging her with impertinent questions about her personal life and her real feelings about him, threatening to use the knife if she didn't answer. Terrified as she was, she did nothing but comment on his double challenge to the relationship; if she answered that would destroy the relationship as they knew and needed it; if he cut himself the session would have to end. Eventually he sat down and could talk about his terror of his own violence, reassured that both of them and the relationship were still intact and could be used to continue the work.

Perhaps another two years later – when the violence was overtly contained, and the primitive confusion had disappeared, and Ted was back in work again living that 'socialized' life he had so rejected in the first letter – he came in with an impish grin and peered closely at her. With a mock rueful sigh he said he had intended to mess around for a bit first, but he could see she was tired and angry (which she was). Something must have gone wrong earlier in the day, and he knew now the only thing to make her wake up and feel happy was a bit of hard work (also true) so he'd forgo the messing around. They both laughed, did some hard work, and he 'messed around' at the end when they could both enjoy it.

The working relationship and the therapeutic alliance can be conceptualized as the framework of the counselling relationship – the conditions necessary for the therapeutic work to go on – although they are clearly part of the work itself and cannot be distinguished neatly from the 'here-and-now' and the 'transference proper'. The last two examples, in fact, illustrate work in the here-and-now. These further two levels in the relationship provide direct information about how the client relates to others and are therefore the meat of the work. Using the relationship as a way of 'doing' counselling, making it the subject of the work, gathering evidence from the dynamics and the process of the interaction is at once the most effective and most parsimonious way of learning about one's internal world. At this point the relationship becomes a technique as well as space for growth.

The here-and-now

The here-and-now refers to what is actually happening in the room in the relationship between the client and counsellor. In their sessions clients mostly recount events from outside the counselling hour: they talk about what happened between themselves and others, about ideas and feelings experienced hours, days or years ago. From these accounts the counsellor can note and comment on patterns of behaviour, feelings, anxieties and defences. Although valuable and essential, all this material has the disadvantage of being remote, somewhat circumstantial, and already reworked in order to be told coherently; and the counsellor's interventions are speculative and necessarily based only on what the client has said. When, however, the same patterns, feelings, anxieties and defences are demonstrated or enacted within the counselling session, the immediacy of the experience and the undeniable evidence of it, before their very eyes, lends conviction and actuality. Because the counsellor is directly involved as a participant and not as a listener, she also has the extra information from her feelings and reactions which can be used to offer the client a fuller picture of why things happen as they do.

Julia repeatedly complained that people around her were saying terrible things about her, accusing her of activities which she vehemently denied. Her counsellor recognized the possibility of malicious gossip, but thought it odd that this pleasant and unassuming girl should attract so much, but they could get nowhere in understanding why this happened, especially since Julia protested innocence for both the alleged activities and any provocation to gossip: she kept herself well to herself and guarded her privacy jealously. But she was a 'hinter' - she alluded to things, seldom giving a full and satisfying description of what went on in her life, leaving the counsellor with speculative ideas and phantasies, some of them none too flattering, to fill in the gaps. While pursuing one such vague reference, she asked a question which Julia construed as a criticism and responded to with the familiar protests of innocence. Given this evidence in the here-and-now, the counsellor was in a good position to point out her tantalizing behaviour and how it actually encouraged others to be curious, to speculate and to enquire. Her distortion of a neutral question into an accusation suggested that she was hiding some shameful ideas and impulses, if not activities. Being unable to acknowledge those guilt-ridden aspects of herself, she managed to get others to express the criticism through her secretive and seductive ways.

That interpersonal dynamic was entirely outside Julia's awareness: she did not realize she hinted, and was at that time quite unconscious of the feelings she was so desperately defending herself against. What she had been able to tell the counsellor about the incidents was, consequently, only part of the story, although it was all of the story so far as she knew. The use of the here-and-now works because people are consistent in their relationships, so they will interact with the counsellor as they interact with everyone else. The client-counsellor relationship becomes a microcosm of other relationships. It is effective because the here-and-now incidents are emotionally alive for both – as opposed to recounted events which are only one person's recollections in relative tranquillity – and the shared subjective experience can be fully exploited for learning about the unconscious component in the client's relationships. A bee flitting from flower to flower does, after all, tell us more about its relationship with its environment than does a dead specimen with pollen on its feet.

The transference

The here-and-now is often called the transference, and it may indeed involve transference phenomena, but, strictly speaking, transference is something else. Transference in one of its forms means that the client is transferring or placing qualities of someone else (usually someone from the past) onto the counsellor and then responding to her as if she were that person. His behaviour is thus inappropriate, an illusion. The unreality of the transference arises from the fact that a past relationship is actually being recreated in the present – not just being remembered or retold – and this results in some perceptual and emotional distortion of the counsellor and the relationship. Generally it is an unconscious process, so the client is not aware of what is happening or what feelings and qualities are being revived. As such it shares much with the here-and-now relationship, but the specificity of the interaction and the persona makes the transference proper. If we take the example used above and pursue it for specific details we can see the transference component.

The 'accusations' made about Julia were primarily that she was trying to create a special relationship with one of her teachers and was also 'cradle-snatching' a young adolescent who was a kind of prodigal son in the school, with sexual designs on both. The accusers were all older women. It was, in fact, unlikely that she was doing either, since she held back from relationships and her sexuality was sternly inhibited. However, it is likely that she may have wanted both. She had been intensely attached to her father as a child, and had been utterly bereft when he died. She badly needed another father. She also had a younger brother, for whom exceptions and special arrangements were made, and whom she consequently resented and bullied. She needed a good relationship with a brother. Her mother was a quiet, rather self-sacrificing woman who seemed to find little pleasure in life. Although she never said anything, Julia was convinced that she was jealous and angry with her for the fun she had with her father. Her anxiety about her impulses and needs in relation to this imagined disapproving mother was surfacing in the closed community of the school and eventually with the counsellor who, in that incident, was treated as if she were Julia's critical mother.

Obviously, as this example shows, transference in its widest sense isn't limited to a therapeutic encounter. It happens all the time in everyday relationships and is often responsible for the confusion that arises when people don't behave as we expect them to (given our past experience) and for the distress that occurs when we have 'made' them behave according to anachronistic models. Within the counselling relationship the transference is the invaluable mechanism which reveals just exactly how the past is all tangled up in the present and creates distortions and pain. It can be used to unravel the web of anxieties and defences which the client brings to his current relationships from the historically defunct, but subjectively contemporary, world of his early relationships, and to demonstrate to him the nature of his current reality. Using the transference is a process of reality testing. Recalling Mark will show how this is so. He attempted to transfer onto his wife and counsellor the qualities of his preoccupied, unreliable mother. His wife accepted and conformed to these attributes, while his counsellor refused to be distorted by the projections and could demonstrate through her consistent and attentive actions that those were not the inevitable attributes of *all* women, so his anger and depression weren't always appropriate. The transference, however, is an extremely powerful dynamic, and because it is unconscious, it isn't always possible for the counsellor to resist the projections.

Edward complained in a panicky but peevish tone that he couldn't possibly prepare for some exams in the time available and intended to withdraw. Previous work had 'explained' what had interfered with his studying, but he asserted that the understanding was useless to him: it had not made him work faster or more effectively. The counsellor was not convinced of the hopelessness of the situation and felt he was copping out; with a slightly peevish edge in her voice she encouraged - perhaps bullied - him to continue. After the session, which he left in defeated defiance, it suddenly occurred to her, with considerable chagrin, that she had responded exactly as his mother always had: forcing him to do what he didn't want to or couldn't do, right to the point of humiliating failure. Her peevishness reflected her annoyance at his denigration of her effort - also horribly familiar. She was also aware of the 'mother knows best' part of her relationship with her own mother.

Some of the power of the transference resides in the fact that the counsellor also brings her independent transference tendencies to the relationship. Clients are also transference objects for her and arouse feelings which are inappropriate to the present relationship. Interference of the counsellor's transference is obviously unhelpful and is prevented by her own awareness of these possibilities through her own therapy or supervision. Different, however, is the counter-transference, which refers to feelings aroused in the counsellor in response to the client's transference. It's as if the unconscious of one speaks to the unconscious of the other in a separate dialogue, which is not specifically linked to the surface topic but which is none the less dynamically relevant. Sometimes this results in a collusion and an unhappy confirmation of a partial and historical reality as if it were the whole and current reality, as it did in Edward's case. The result need not always be disastrous; in fact, it is part of the basic empathy which is necessary to the work, an expression of being closely in touch with the client and his feelings. But the counter-transference is most useful when the counsellor is aware of it and can use it as a tool, just as the transference is used to lift the interaction into the sphere of conscious dialogue and learning.

In addition to transference as the projection of a past image or relationship onto a present one, complete with feelings associated with that image, there is the transference of feelings and impulses. Here the client denies and disowns an unwelcome feeling within himself and attributes it to the counsellor in an attempt to put an end to some internal discomfort or conflict. A sign for the counsellor that this is happening is that she has a mood change in the middle of a session for 'no good reason' in terms of herself and her internal state. Clients dump their unwanted feelings and feel that much lighter, leaving the counsellor that much heavier.

Tom was describing some changes at work. He was mildly sarcastic about the intelligence behind the changes and was planning how he could organize himself to continue his work despite the inconveniences caused by the changes. As he chatted on quite equitably, the counsellor suddenly felt furious. She could see that the change amounted to messing him about quite seriously, and were just cause for anger. He, however, denied any anger – he never got angry, there was no point, it didn't change anything; angry people frightened him anyway.

Another sign is the emergence of a fruitless argument between client and counsellor, in which each expresses and argues for one half of a conflict or an ambivalent state in the client. Eleanor was a past-master at this. She could easily inveigle her counsellor into a debate about whether or not she was 'getting better'. She would lament that nothing was happening, and the counsellor would reply with a list of evidence that things had changed. One expressed depression over what had been given up through change and what still needed to be done; the other a sense of achievement over some improvement in her life. The fruitful response would have been to recognize Eleanor's conflict over change, and so have her take back what she had projected in order to work on her internal struggle. Feelings and impulses need to be put back where they belong – in the client – in order to prevent emotional poverty within him and to help him explore why some feelings need to be repudiated and dumped elsewhere.

Transference is mostly unconscious and becomes known through the sensation of incongruity. When the client is relating to the counsellor as if she were someone else, or loads her with his feelings, she feels uncomfortable and wants to protest 'but this isn't me'. Through not reasserting herself immediately, but letting the transference develop, both can gain emotional understanding about the kinds of phantasies and feelings which the client invests in his relationships and why he has to distort his world in that particular way. While the client elaborates his transference relationships, the counsellor holds on to her counter-transference as silent and invisible material. Through the transference relationship, the client has the opportunity to rework old relationships in a benign and mutative environment so that he may ultimately relinquish them to his memory.

There is probably no way to describe accurately and adequately the counselling relationship and its myriad facets. The different levels - play, exploration, work, the alliance, the here-and-now and transference - may be discriminated, but they interweave with each other to create a personal encounter which is unique and greater than the sum of its parts.

5 ‖ The language of counselling

Psycho-therapeutic counselling relies heavily on words. Happily our language and speech are highly complex and subjectively rich, affording plenty of opportunities for both literal and emotional communication. We each use our language in a very individual, if not idiosyncratic, way but beyond the special quality of the words, statements and stories themselves, the context in which we speak also lends them a particular significance; conversely, language becomes an invaluable source of clues about our internal world. The 'Freudian slip', no doubt familiar to all, demonstrates how what we intend to say is sometimes different from what we really think and feel. In a similar but broader way, what we say, when and where we say it, the particular content and words chosen, all offer glimpses of otherwise concealed attitudes, assumptions and feelings. The 'slip' has unfortunately acquired overtones of betrayal, and it is true that language and speech are structures for containing anxiety and conflict and can be dispassionately dismantled to expose raw patches. However, they are also an integral part of identity and deserve respect. The counsellor listens carefully to the emotional and contextual messages to comprehend the personal meaning within the conversational exchange. This furthers the therapeutic aim exactly as understanding the transference does. Ordinarily language is outside conscious awareness – either because we learnt it unwittingly and it has become habitual, or because it is backed by motives which are themselves unconscious – but in counselling, with the counsellor's observations and feedback, the client has a unique chance to hear himself speaking.

THE PERSONAL MEANING OF LANGUAGE

Our individual style of speaking – our words, voice and expression – is a crucial part of our social identity; the success of character impersonators attests to that. Because this style is fundamentally shaped by cultural and family settings, it is also a central part of our personal identity and associates us with specific groups of people. Through experience we acquire a vocabulary for organizing and identifying the world around us. The more we have been able to observe and discriminate, the richer our world; the more ways we have of categorizing and organizing our world, the more varied our vocabulary. This in itself may, of course, become part of our identity – someone whose speech is pedestrian, or brightened by metaphor, or painfully precise; someone who can name all the different kinds of butterfly, or for whom all insects are just bugs. Through experience also we gain different perspectives on situations and learn different ways of naming the same thing. The lady in the schoolroom, for instance, may be 'Teacher', but she may also be an 'old bag'. We learn not to call her 'old bag' at home, nor to call her 'teacher' among disaffected schoolmates; only if very angry are we likely to call her 'old bag' to her face. It's only a short step from using words judiciously in order to belong to a particular group to using them consciously to evoke particular responses in others, as do comedians, preachers and campaigners. We may do exactly the same things without knowing it, however, and here we are concerned with the client's capacity to speak, quite unconsciously, about his inner self through ordinary speech.

Because our language expresses our identity, a client's use of personal pronouns reveals much about his sense of himself. These two people would never call themselves 'I'.

A young boy, whose Christian names were Martin Luther King, always used the third person objective to refer to himself: 'Him done it'; 'Him went to school'; 'Him wants a lolly'. In all other respects his speech was reasonably grammatical, and he was bright, so this peculiarity was undoubtedly psychological in origin. His mother idolized King, who died just before Martin was born, and there were already four children, so he was treated rather as a (dead) object in that relationship – and so he represented himself linguistically.

Ruth was a very capable nurse who used 'one': 'One does want to be kind.' 'One has a great deal of responsibility.' She would respond more readily to 'Sister' than to Ruth. She justified this in terms of being a nurse who had to keep her distance in order to tolerate the stresses of work, but the usage spilled into her personal life. Her difficulty in taking responsibility for herself and her relationships was evidenced by constant conflict between being a wife and nurse and by a terrible restlessness about where and how to use her skills.

Other language and speech characteristics can express difficulties around a client's sense of himself. Examples are endless, but the meaning is always idiosyncratic. One young man began nearly every sentence with 'I' as if he needed to remind everyone that he did still exist; a girl with the same habit did so to remind others that she should be the centre of the universe. At the other end of the spectrum are people who circumvent any direct reference to themselves. One could speak of himself only through the characters he identified with in the book he was reading because his anxiety in the face-to-face encounter paralysed him, and without a vehicle for talking about himself he had to be silent. A similar kind of avoidance in 'I have a friend who . . .', is more transparent and needs to be decoded and responsibility put gently back to the client, lest the underlying problem of shame is compounded. Another subtle means of talking about the unconscious self is to talk about somebody else.

Barbara regularly complained about her greedy, lazy, envious, self-pitying, inconsiderate and infuriating flatmate, but she did nothing about the intolerable situation. Gradually it became clear that she feared all these despised qualities were lurking inside her hard-working, martyrish, polite personality, and she needed the flatmate as someone to hate in preference to despising herself.

Whenever a client takes up a disproportionate amount of time and energy in talking about someone else, it's quite probable that he is discussing some aspect of himself which he cannot acknowledge or confront.

Finally, two foreigners illustrate how words give clues to problems about the self which are difficult to manage.

Jonathan was too embarrassed to say directly why he had come. He shuffled around verbally in very sophisticated English, but was quite unaware of confusion in his use of 'he' and 'she'. From this and his awkwardness the counsellor could speculate, correctly and to his relief, that he was confused about his sexual identity.

The other was also fluent in English, but hopelessly tangled up his prepositions - that part of speech which states the relationship between two things. These are realistically difficult and arbitrary in and between languages, but he was unduly upset by getting them wrong so often and would exclaim in exasperation that he was no better at prepositions than he was at his relationships with women - he was at, on, with, or in them, when he should be doing something else to - or is it with? - them.

In everyday communication we tend to use words, particularly adjectives and adverbs, imprecisely. We describe things as 'super', 'terrific', 'awful', 'beautiful' or 'dreadful', trusting that the listener has a similar vocabulary and will understand accurately enough. We use such common words because they are vague and effortless and don't require difficult evaluation. A challenge to be more specific can generate mild alarm or even despair as often we don't know what we really do mean; or it suited us to be ambiguous. Usually understanding is approximate enough for communication to continue, but sometimes it is important to extract a more precise meaning from the protective cover of a well-worn expression. Most diagnostic words, for example, are now in common parlance, and clients will label themselves depressed, paranoid, schizophrenic or phobic, using the words in ways which would seem novel or downright inaccurate to a clinician, so it is important to find out exactly what they mean.

Clichés also often need translating. Many adolescents will say, at some time, 'My parents don't understand', and that can mean anything from true communication breakdown to parental disapproval. Similarly, job-hunters will designate something as 'unsuitable' which may mean 'I don't like it', 'I can't do it', 'I don't really want to change jobs' or even 'God says I shouldn't'. This last came from a devout fundamentalist who had put his career decisions in God's hands. He believed that God would put obstacles in the way of jobs he shouldn't have. Lack of success meant that God didn't want him to have that job. On the other hand, specific words, because of the objects or experiences they represent, sometimes are highly idiosyncratic keys or passwords to an immense area of feelings and memories. Proust's *petite madelaine* is probably the best known of these, but each person has his own emotional lexicon. 'Kipper' was a key word for Mark. A tremendous row had developed over who would prepare the kippers for Sunday breakfast, and the fish were ultimately mangled. A treat had become a sore subject, and the incident itself had been burdened with all his lifetime's disappointment and resentments. Afterwards, the word and the fish automatically evoked these feelings and were used as a shorthand to describe them. No word is 'just a word', and some are bigger than others.

Sometimes, though, symbolic quality of words breaks down, and the speaker has the illusion that uttering a word is equal to doing it, for better or worse:

> Frank had occasional bouts of severe depression and anxiety. He would come to the counsellor's office to sit with her while he rid himself of the feelings, commenting on the process: 'The depression is a big weight on my shoulders. I shrug and it falls off. I put my thoughts in a plastic sack and throw it away. I grind them up with this steel frame. I crush them with this clamp.' And he would leave, feeling all right again.

This is an extreme example. It is more common that the omnipotence-based anxiety in using, or even thinking, a word or thought results in avoiding it altogether lest it come true in reality. This is especially so if the thought is about harm to another person. These very concrete or symbolic usages of words and language are often responsible for learning difficulties: the anxiety surrounding them disrupts the concentration and objectivity necessary to take in the 'facts'.

The apparently dreary matter of grammar is also a rich source of clues about the client, because it is so complex and is used so 'naturally' by every one of us. Whether correct or not, the grammatical structure used by a client expresses something of his internal world and his relationships. Through the parts of speech, tenses, cases, voices, punctuations and constructions, the English language offers a variety of modes for expressing and communicating experience accurately. Very few people, however, exploit that variety; they characteristically favour one form of expression, and the choices and limitations are likely to be personally significant. Some people speak in present tense verbs, in the active voice; others use nouns and the passive voice. The difference in listening to them is like the difference between watching cine-film and looking at snapshots, and hints at how they manage the liveliness of experience. Some speak sparsely in skeletal sentences; others use elaborate constructions and litter their sentences with adjectives. They may be just stating what is or describing and qualifying; they may be conveying that the world is drab or rich, sufficient in itself or needing to be dressed up in mellifluous prose. Some people use punctuation sensitively: others use only conjunctions, breathlessly connecting everything together. Some never finish sentences; others end with vocal lift as if everything is a question; others have a free-floating use of he, she and it. All these verbal clues raise questions about how the speakers relate to others, and how committed they are to what they say. The possibilities are as endless in variety as grammar is, and these general observations serve only to point to the value of noticing linguistic habits and deviations from the usual, and especially any change in use of language which often reflects an internal shift.

CONTEXTUAL CLUES: SELECTION, SEQUENCE AND TIMING

While the client has his idiosyncrasies of speech and language, his position as client in a counselling relationship will influence what he says and how he says it. An element of selection and conscious or unconscious intention is present and necessary. Most obviously, since he comes as someone with a problem in need of help, his communications tend to be ones which elaborate or elucidate the problem. He is more likely to mention what's gone wrong than what's gone right in his life. Hence the picture is partial. Conversely, the counsellor is biased to listen for what has 'mishappened' and may not attend so closely to the successes in the client's experience (notwithstanding that much can be learnt from understanding why things go well). Over time both learn the language of the other, and a mutually useful and acceptable verbal currency develops. This more emotional language is often quite specific to the relationship, and may seldom be used elsewhere.

The counselling session itself provides a framework which structures and gives additional meaning to the content: it is time-limited, has a beginning and an end, and is usually one of a series. It is never possible to relate everything that has happened in a lifetime, a week, or a day, so if only an hour is available, a high degree of selection is necessary. A variety of criteria can be used: a dominating internal or external event in the past or near future; a quick resumé and commentary on 'everything' that has happened; the symptom; what happened on the way to the session; something apparently trivial but fascinating; it can be planned beforehand or left to spontaneous inspiration. Whatever they are, both the criteria and the products of the selection are meaningful above and beyond the content. The girl who always began with a resumé of her week did so in order to remember 'all of me' before concentrating on one aspect of herself; the man who rehearsed what he would say revealed his anxiety about losing control; any person who talks however inconsequently about clothes or cats or clouds is talking about them because they, or what they represent, matter to him. Out of the thousands of things to choose from, whether he chose consciously or 'fortuitously', he did select them and that cannot be irrelevant. Even chattering to postpone a difficult topic may actually be leading up to the topic:

> Cathy began a session by describing, in a depressed way, how she failed to see the meaning of a film she had seen with a friend, who understood it deeply. And she had been to a dinner-party, during which she felt stupid because she didn't know everything about politics and economics. Next she reported that her mother's operation had been postponed at the last minute, and her mother had become disoriented and distressed. And the flat she was sure she was going to get had fallen through, also at the last minute. After each bit of information she had asked herself why she was saying all this. Finally she spoke of her doubts about a course she had just begun. Should she do it? Would she be able to finish it? Through the various items she was building toward the theme of fearing that opportunities would be snatched from her, and was that because she was too inadequate to deserve them in the first place?

Choosing to omit things may also be relevant and purposeful, but that is harder to know and can only be deduced from the context or from the counsellor's uneasy sense of incompleteness or unmet expectations. If, for instance, a client spends most of a session untangling his anxiety about an imminent event, but then doesn't mention the event later, he probably has some reason not to do so. Failure to mention something which is known to be important is also always noteworthy.

> Kate was very sensitive about her birthday; it mattered intensely that her friends remembered and celebrated it. In the session after her birthday she talked at excessive length about a minor snub at work which had depressed her disproportionately. The counsellor began to suspect that her birthday had gone badly, and that this other incident was being burdened with her disappointment. She commented on this and learnt that the celebrations had been perfunctory, but Kate had felt it was too childish to complain. Through discussing this they arrived at Kate's distress over feeling she was an unwanted child – a feeling which invaded all her relationships and made her too vulnerable to the slightest neglect or criticism.

Often the omission isn't so easy to identify, but the counsellor may feel there is a missing piece needed to connect and make sense of all the other pieces. A comment based on this feeling frequently prompts the client to 'remember' what he had left out.

The order in which ideas follow each other is also significant and, along with the selection of topics, provides clues about unconscious preoccupations. The sequence is not random; it is created by the client's need to develop and explore a particular theme. 'Free association' is free only in the sense that there is no conscious censorship; it is strongly determined from inside. The underlying meaning may take a long time to reveal itself, and it may require all the contextual cues available to make it intelligible. The counsellor also has to allow her thoughts to range around the topics to find connections; her free associations are relevant to the degree that she has become engrossed in the client's current subjective reality. This process has already been illustrated by Cathy's collection of ideas, but in this example the contributions of both client and counsellor (her unspoken thoughts are in brackets) are given to demonstrate the joint endeavour to find the meaning in the sequence of communications. The counsellor sits it out, aside from a few neutral comments, until the message is more or less complete.

> Ted sits in the chair facing her. (He has a choice of four seats – each has gradually acquired a known meaning: that he is feeling bad, mad,

sad or glad. This is the 'bad' one. Is he angry, naughty?) He begins by saying, gruffly, that he feels different today. (Different from usual, from others?) After a pause while he looks around, he comments on a statistics book, wondering if she uses it, and discourses somewhat scornfully on probability, false logic and artifacts. (The book has always been there, so this theme must be relevant. Statistics submerge the individual into the general, he becomes a cipher?) He continues the subject of false logic by recounting an argument with a friend about the earth and moon. It isn't true that only the earth rotates - the moon does too - but his friend was convinced that the moon couldn't move. (The moon and earth are interdependent - the tides - but they are also autonomous. Is this argument his internal conflict about dependence and independence?)

He yawns and says he didn't sleep last night; it was too hot and he hasn't managed to regulate the heat in his new flat. (Dependence-independence again. His recent rehousing by the Council coincides with a proposed move of her office. Change always upsets him - the heat is on metaphorically?) He wants to make some changes in the flat but can't start because he doesn't know how long he'll stay - the Social Services are messing him around about his dole. (Can he make his mark and be an individual or is he always dependent on external forces? What will happen to him when she moves? He tends to feel helpless against faceless organizations.) He gives a despairing and angry account of the stupid lady at the Job Centre who doesn't see any problem in asking him to leave his home area to work in another part of the country. (Same message, more strongly. He feels no one takes his individual needs into account, but he is anxious about asserting himself because he is dependent on these powerful others. The two moves have highlighted his conflict between autonomy and dependence. He feels fixed while others come and go.) She interprets his anxiety about being left behind when others move and his anger toward those, including herself, who remind him of his dependence. He says he has worried that she will stop the meetings when she moves. He wants to be the one to leave, but he isn't ready to go, and he hates feeling so threatened by others who always seem to have power over him.

These odd bits of related experience fall into a pattern and the pattern in turn gives meaning to the individual bits of experiences within the overall emotional texture of the client's life. Ted had been abandoned by both parents at different times in his childhood, and he kept returning in his life and in the sessions to the theme of anger, hurt and fear about desertion.

It will be evident that the sequence of topics provides valuable clues only if the counsellor is able to keep quiet and allow the client to organize and construct his messages as he will. Interrupting or redirecting ideas and feelings spoils both the development and the usefulness of the material. It is this which distinguishes the counselling dialogue from ordinary conversation; in the to and fro of conversation each tends to reply to the last thing said, while the counsellor responds to an accumulation of messages.

The timing of communications is dynamically determined just as selection and sequence are, and the chronology of the session may be directly used by the client to say something about himself. The fact of a beginning and an end makes it easy for a client to talk about what it means to start, stop or interrupt a relationship or a piece of work, and how he manages the time boundaries reveals aspects of his feelings and behaviour which he might be unaware of.

Kate always came into the room talking and left it talking. No actual time boundary seemed to exist for her, and the counsellor felt deliberately excluded, made to pick up the thread of a conversation and then leave it midstream. Kate was a needy and controlling girl, and she resented the strict time limit. She had an hour's journey to and from the session. So she effectively had a three-hour session during which she had an actual counsellor only for the middle hour; she made up a dialogue for the other two hours. She would begin and end in her own time, not someone else's. Time-keeping was a perpetual problem for her, and by doing some here-and-now work on time in the session, she understood the reasons for her disguised hostility and recognized that she could choose to be on time as well as late or early elsewhere.

By contrast, Mandy, who was something of a Cinderella in her life, treated the beginning and end like magic points of transformation She always knew the accurate time and came and went precisely with the clock, hardly permitting herself a hello or goodbye outside the hour. The work with Mandy concentrated on her feeling that she had no right to anything from others and anything 'extra' would be begrudged. Exploration of her management of the time boundaries helped her to see that the rigidity and 'miserliness' lay within herself and not in others.

These two girls had very different relationships with time, but almost everyone has an internal sense of time, according to which they wittingly or unwittingly pace their communications through the sessions. Mandy managed to conclude what she had to say with seconds to spare in a manoeuvre which was almost elegant, and her final chunk usually symbolically concerned ending and conveyed her particular feeling about stopping on that day: relief, frustration, satisfaction, anger, cliff-hanging. This 'ending with ending' happens with fascinating frequency even in those not so conscious of time. The pacing occurs throughout sessions, individually or in series, and the subjective sense of time will influence how the client uses the time available: there may be 'plenty of time' to explore something thoroughly or to put it off for a while; or time may be 'running out', so a sense of urgency or pointlessness will influence the work. When a topic is introduced, therefore, can indicate something of its place in the client's hierarchy of priorities and anxieties.

The very first communication usually deserves close attention because it often sets the tone and theme for all that follows, although this isn't always immediately obvious. In the case of the man who arrived late for his first meeting and complained about getting lost in the building because the signs were inadequate, however, all the immediate signs of confusion, dependence and angry resistance to self-motivated work were confirmed again and again. The final words, the 'doorknob communication', also tend to be important because they may refer to a feeling or subject which the client wants, but is afraid to explore. Because they are said on the way out, the client doesn't have to follow them through or face the consequences. The impact of doorknob communications is often tremendous because the counsellor is left with the anxiety, especially if it is the only (and often it is a favourite) way a client can show his anger with the counsellor about the ending of the meeting.

The counselling sessions will acquire a particular place among all the events in the client's life, and this will influence how he regards the breaks and the continuation, which in turn says something about how he feels about the work and relationships generally. With those who become very involved in the counselling, the breaks, especially long ones, tend to arouse anger and anxiety as the natural feelings of a frustrated attachment or dependence. Knowing the value of the sessions for a particular client often helps to understand what goes on within and even outside the meetings. In some cases, the week may be subjectively reorganized to accommodate the feelings of uplift, pensiveness or depression which surround the sessions; other relationships or activities, especially those immediately before or after, may be invaded by feelings belonging to the session.

EMOTIONAL FILTERS

Finally, fully understanding what the client is communicating depends on appreciating the current emotional state of the relationship. It has already been noted that what is said is influenced by the mere fact that they are client and counsellor in a counselling relationship. Clients have assumptions and expectations about the meetings, and their explanations about why they've come often reveal their attitude toward seeking help (from others besides the counsellor as well) and that will influence the work heavily. They may be hostile – a sullen 'I was sent'; ambivalent – 'I don't know where to begin, but I'm glad I got myself here'; or hopeful – 'You helped my friend.' Right from the beginning, the nature of the communication says much about the client.

These assumptions at the outset immediately establish a transference relationship and provide an opportunity to look at how the client copes with his feelings about needing help and being emotionally understood. Throughout the work the transference will change but it will always be there, so it is important to know who, psychologically speaking, is talking to whom, because this will affect how things are heard and said. Particularly when the transference is strong and may be supplanting the reality of those two people in that room, the actual interchange may be transformed as it is experienced in the unconscious relationship. Something similar to this has probably been experienced by most people when, for instance, they have reacted quite differently to exactly the same piece of criticism when it is given by a friend and then by a superior. Any conversation is open to the hazard of a double-level interchange, and it is often difficult to evaluate dialogues recounted by a client. In this example, however, it is evident that the people (or more accurately, the client's view of them) giving information influenced the value of the information and confused him.

Ralph was trying to decide between accountancy and marketing as a career, and he spoke to men established in both areas. The accountants had given him an attractive picture of their work and mentioned skills and qualities which he had and enjoyed – but it wasn't appealing to him. The marketing men, on the other hand, had frightened him with job requirements which were totally alien to his personality and capabilities – but he was drawn to it. It emerged that all the accountants had been fat, middle-aged and balding while the marketing men were young, dynamic and handsome. The accountancy image was intolerable, the marketing image desirable, and that over-shadowed the content of the professions.

Within the counselling relationship, something said by the counsellor as herself may be accepted as it is given, but in so far as it is also 'spoken' by the counsellor in a transference role, it is heard quite differently with different consequences.

Barry had placed his counsellor in the role of a woman passionately in love with him – a combination of wish fulfilment and a transference from his early entranced relationship with his mother. He, of course, was the irresistible lover in that relationship. While establishing the practicalities of the work, apparently all reality-based, she gave him her 'phone number, as was her custom with all clients. Later, when every friendly remark she made was interpreted by him as a breakdown of her 'professionally necessary resistance' to his charms, he astonished her by saying that giving him her number was incontrovertible evidence of her passion for him.

Another way of expressing this problem in communication is to say than what is given out and taken in passes through emotional filters, and each filter alters the communication according to its own nature. People in their real and transference aspects are one sort of filter; emotional states and motivations are others.

Moods which come and go have a superficial and obvious effect on communication for only as long as they last. More persistent and entrenched emotional states or personal qualities, however, can profoundly affect the work, even to the point of stopping it altogether. A client who is in a primitive persecuted state, when he feels the whole world is attacking him, is bound to interpret his counsellor's efforts as attacks as well. Through the 'either-or' dynamic which identifies her as wholly 'bad', anything which comes from her is also bad and has to be rejected or destroyed. Those who are deeply humiliated by the need for counselling, or are envious or frightened of the counsellor's capacity to understand and articulate their feelings, also are driven to attack the communication process and the words themselves. At times they will argue, question, split hairs, and virtually dismember everything she has said to prove she is silly and useless. The uncontrollable need to spoil the very thing they need and are asking for must become the focus of the work, but of course attempts to elucidate this are subject to the same destructiveness. It is frustrating and discouraging for both sides, and the situation is saved only by a good therapeutic alliance.

Every communication contains a test of the other's willingness to understand. The underlying intention to understand makes the test less difficult. Sometimes, however, what we are intended to understand is far from straightforward. The speaker may want to create a mood or evoke a particular emotional response in his listener, and the spoken 'facts' are merely a means to that end. A client may try to gain a response he needs emotionally, trying to push the counsellor into a transference role complementary to the one he wishes to take up.

> Edward had phases of being really disagreeable, hoping to make his counsellor nasty in return so he could sustain his pathetic complaint that people always picked on him – a dynamic from the boyhood relationship with his brother which is still unresolved.

Others seem to want the counsellor to know what it feels like to be them, and so do to the counsellor what others have done to them. Sometimes this has an additional 'poor me' overlay, by which the client hopes the counsellor will fail to see how the client himself provokes or maintains the distressing situation. They don't want to be understood because that would mean having to take personal responsibility for their circumstances. Another more subtle way of impeding understanding is to be ironic or sarcastic, so real feelings are obscured; usually this means that feelings have at one time been the cause of humiliation or punishment. These motivated messages and the intention to create feelings or distractions in others are not usually calculated and, even if they distort reality, they are not deliberately false.

THE PROBLEM OF TRUTH

This raises the problem of truth in counselling. We know from philosophy and psychology that no event is experienced by two people in exactly the same way. Eye-witnesses' accounts always vary in significant details, because they all saw the event from a different physical position and were sensitive to different facets of the event; they describe it in the light of what it felt like to be part of it.

> While giving a recital, Julia had to start a piece again because a string slipped. Her story was that she lost her nerve, never became involved in the music and gave an uninspired performance. A critic commented that she recovered well from an unfortunate beginning and went on to give a subtly underplayed and very moving performance.

We see the world through our own eyes, conditioned by experience and by our immediate internal state. The inherent biases are mostly outside awareness. Our memory of the past is subject to these same selections and distortions, and, to compound the ambiguity, every time we recount an event we tell it slightly differently according to whichever cues and context have reminded us of it. Past and present, there is no perception without interpretation. The subjective reality is as important as the actuality, and it is, in fact, the 'malleability' of our perception of events which makes internal change possible at all.

A client, in telling his story, presents his own reality. It may not match up with how things actually were or are: the chronology might defy the clock and calendar; the account of people, places, thoughts and feelings might be glaringly inconsistent, but, in the words of one client: 'If it's in my mind, it's real.' Perhaps it should eventually be straightened out, but the counsellor accepts the given version for the time being and explores it to understand the client's need to structure or recount his experience in that way.

Dorothy had been a passenger in a car which hit and killed an old woman. The driver had been acquitted, but she still felt they were guilty – even if the woman had stepped directly in the path of the car, they should have been watching more carefully. The problem for her was to separate her objective (and healthy) guilt toward this woman from her irrational guilt about angry and destructive feelings toward her mother which had been stirred up by the accident. The counselling task was not to make a legal decision about culpability, but to deal with the emotional consequences of the accident and the judgement.

Truth is, after all, difficult: it is hard to speak the exact truth even if no falsehood is intended. The attempt to be honest with oneself in the presence of another inevitably calls upon the exhibitionist tendency of the teller to satisfy the voyeuristic tendency of the hearer. Facts, sadly, rarely meet the requirements of our beliefs and needs, and it is tempting to elaborate them a bit.

THE COUNSELLOR'S COMMUNICATIONS

It will be evident by now that if the client's best ally in counselling is the ability to speak freely and emotionally of himself and his experience, the counsellor's is her ability to listen, because most of what she says is based on what she has heard. But she is not simply absorbing it, sponge-fashion. As all the examples so far illustrate, while she listens, she evaluates what she hears in terms of what she knows about the client, the relationship and the nature of communication. In a sense, she metabolizes the material and gives it back to the client in a form which is more useful to him than it was originally. As one client put it; 'If you don't see it differently from how I do, you are useless to me.' Her intervention can take many forms: she may interpret, make links, clarify, confront or teach. But it should always invite movement: release feelings, unjam a blockage, unravel defences, lift unconscious feelings into awareness, direct attention to a fruitful or avoided area. It can concern anything that occurs within the relationship: the content, the process, the transference; but its effectiveness resides in its immediacy. To promote movement an intervention capitalizes on the client's emotional involvement and his anxiety. It must be given when the client is ready to hear and use it, so here, too, timing is of the essence.

Often it isn't necessary for the counsellor to say much at all. If the client is listening to himself (and, after all, it is he, above anyone else, who should hear himself), is emotionally in touch with himself, and is relatively free from defensiveness then he can do for himself most of what a counsellor can do. It is enough that she is a witness.

Roger came feeling desperately confused and panicky about a job decision. He had rehearsed all the arguments but couldn't make up his mind. With the counsellor he rehearsed them again, and the choice was obvious 'Why', he asked, 'is it that when I talk to you – but really I've only been talking to myself and you're just here – my thoughts seem so reasonable? I think it is because you're so still and that makes me calm.'

By contrast, Mark, who was in a similar position, and had weighed up all the pros and cons, was going around in circles of indecision and escalating his anxiety. It seemed to the counsellor that the problem wasn't that one job might be better than another, but that the need to decide was 'wrong'. She put that to him, and he agreed that it wasn't fair to have to lose one job by choosing the other. Only when they had taken account of this could he finally make a decision.

In this second example, the counsellor's contribution was to see through the muddle and redefine the problem so that it could be more constructively tackled. Clarification helps those who seem unable to say what they want to say or who are tangled up in their own confusion; fairly aggressive confrontation is sometimes useful in the face of bloody-mindedness or unconvincing helplessness; and some explanation about people and relationships may enlighten a bewildered client who seems to have no framework for thinking about himself. The counsellor's major contribution, however, is to work with the client's unconscious messages which he, by definition, cannot immediately know: her interpretation begins where he leaves off or where his defences prevent him from going.

An interpretation intends to 'explain' overt behaviour and feelings by referring to the hidden feelings, anxieties, defences and phantasies. The same theoretical structures used for psycho-dynamic diagnosis are used for formulating an interpretation. Using the impulse-anxiety-defence model, the counsellor observes that the client feels, or wants to act on, an impulse (he is angry), but that wish makes him anxious (he is afraid of hurting someone), so he mobilizes a defence to allay the anxiety (he does the opposite and is excessively pleasant). Using Ezriel's formulation, the client enters in a required relationship (he ignores the girl he fancies) in order not to have the avoided relationship (sexual) which he imagines will result in catastrophe (she will reject his advances outright). Strachey (1934) further stipulated that an interpretation should refer to the transference and current relationships and link them to historical precedents. (You agree with me and submit to your friend's plans because you are afraid we shall be angry if you don't, as if we were your father who had to be appeased.) At one level, developing an interpretation is an intellectual process for the counsellor, but if it is to be effective it must be supported by the counsellor's feelings and refer directly to the client's immediate feelings and anxieties. For this reason, interpretations based on evidence from the here-and-now or the transference are most likely to make an emotional impact and lead to change.

Whatever form the counsellor's intervention takes, there are three golden rules which are essential to observe in putting anything to the client about himself, his behaviour or his feelings. The first is that a counsellor can never know anything about her client with absolute certainty. The evidence may be plentiful, but because so much comes from subjective areas, she can only offer an informed hypothesis for the client to respond to. The all-knowing counsellor who pronounces from on high fundamentally offends the integrity of her client and their relationship. The second is that any intervention must have a 'because' clause. Clients on the whole have a good idea about *what* they do; they need help with the *why*. Furthermore, just saying that they are doing this or that runs the risk of sounding, and actually being, ungenerously judgemental. Finally, it is the underlying feelings which are important and need to be mobilized. What has been cannot be changed or eradicated, but feelings can, and consequently they are the key to change. These three rules exist because they ensure the client space to manoeuvre after an intervention. Regardless of how positively given and received, an intervention is a threat to the existing self: it intends to create change, it presents the client with something he has been protecting himself against, and it reminds him of his vulnerability in needing someone to see what he hasn't been able to see for himself. To make him a prisoner of his own communications and his willingness to change is, to say the least, unfair.

6 | Authority and responsibility in counselling

Counselling cannot be undertaken lightly: it entails responsibility and integrity in the counsellor, and it promises a variety of anxious moments as ethical, moral, legal and even mortal matters emerge. Some prior consideration of her assumptions, aims and principles about the work can avert the worst of the anxieties, but, more important, it contributes to her authority as a counsellor: her right and confidence to counsel. Prior consideration, however, is not sufficient: her style of work will inevitably develop in the course of experience, and each client is likely to touch her uniquely. Both call for continuous reassessment of what, how and why she does what she does.

BEGINNING AND ENDING

When a counsellor undertakes work with a client, she implicitly accepts some responsibility for him, herself and their shared environment, but there are few guidelines or codes of behaviour which define the content or limits of such accountability. The least to be said is that she will not abuse the individuality and vulnerability of the client and will do whatever is within her capacity (since she is human) to create conditions for growth and change, and that responsibility begins from the moment of meeting a potential client and ends only when the work is terminated. Certainly the decision about whether she should counsel someone is hers. This decision is practical, personal and emotional. During the initial meeting - and perhaps before that, at the point of referral - the counsellor uses all her diagnostic skills to assess the person's needs and his readiness and suitability for counselling and her kind of counselling in particular. Simultaneously she reviews whether she has the skills and resources for the work required. This involves discovering as much as she can about the client's problems, his current circumstances and his story in order to think about the length and depth of counselling ahead. His motivation and expectations are revealed through what he says about them and how he responds in the here-and-now to her responses and her explanations about how she understands and works at counselling. It is also prudent to discover whether other professionals are, or have been, involved with him, since it is untherapeutic and bad etiquette to interfere with work already under way. It is responsible to accept a client only when the counsellor is reasonably certain that he understands what he is entering into and is doing so voluntarily, with realistic expectations, and the intention and resilience to work; and when she is equally confident that she has a good idea about the work to be done, has the skills to match his therapeutic needs, and has the time and energy and willingness to do it. Obviously the more alert she is to transference and counter-transference feelings as well as factual and practical data, the better grounded her decision will be. So that they both know where they stand with each other, a contract about time – either a definite number of sessions or an exploratory phase and then review – and whatever rules the counsellor may have about their behaviour with each other within and around the sessions should be clearly stated and agreed between them.

Decisions about continuing or ending involve much the same issues. The counsellor will be considering and discussing whether the work done is sufficient or whether the next phase should be embarked upon, whether she is still functioning within her skills, and whether it is appropriate to continue. An extended counselling relationship can become a ritualized and defensive retreat from the ordinary business of living, resulting in stagnation or the client's reluctance to venture out on his own to test out his growth and resources without a counsellor in the background. If that is so, then it is time to plan to end, with a termination date set far enough ahead to give them time to work on the ending itself. Difficult as it is, a counsellor must always be prepared to acknowledge that either she can't help, is out of her depth, or is no longer needed.

The arrangements are seldom ideal; usually there has to be a compromise between what is needed and what is available. Even so, they should be mutually agreed, but it is not uncommon for the client to feel that the counsellor is always in a position to decide whether she gives or withholds the 'goodies' he wants, and the question of power is always latent in the relationship. Certainly the counselling relationship often feels – and is – very powerful because of the intense feelings and interactions which emerge and affect the two people, especially when the transference is strong. Such force is legitimate, and even necessary for change to occur, but it also gives rise to phantasies and anxieties about manipulation and exploitation. These are all the more troublesome because psychological harm is so subtle and idiosyncratic: our daily lives relentlessly remind us of what people can do to each other despite best intentions or through simply 'not thinking'.

MODELS OF HELPFULNESS

The strongly emotional debate between theoretical schools about the effectiveness of different therapeutic models in terms of cures, failures and explanatory power are, at one level, exactly like the rival claims of two soap powders, but at another level they reflect an underlying anxiety about whether the work is really harmful or helpful. Within the counselling world the principal debate seems to be between the directive and non-directive stances. Some further aspects of responsibility in counselling can be looked at by considering the implications of the assumptions and aims of these theoretical positions.

'Directive' and 'non-directive' are perhaps misleading in this context since 'non-directive' already has a meaning traditionally associated with the form of counselling developed by Carl Rogers. Here the terms are used more generally to denote the degree of involvement – both the degree to which the counsellor becomes directly involved in the client's life and activity, and the extent to which she overtly calls on and voices her experience, personality and feelings in the therapeutic interaction. At one extreme of the directive position is the counsellor who advises clients about what to do, how to do it, perhaps even how to think and feel, frequently using herself as an explicit reference point. The 'blank screen' counsellor, who remains aloof from the practicalities of the client's life and concentrates on his internal and unconscious world in the transference, falls at the extreme of the non-directive position. The majority of counsellors place themselves somewhere in the middle, and are flexible to accommodate the requirements of a particular client's objectives and needs. Identifiable, but not necessarily conscious, assumptions about the nature of the client's needs, and the aim of the counselling relationship, are likely to be operating at each end of the continuum.

At the directive end is the assumption that the client doesn't have adequate or appropriate resources, or cannot mobilize them and so needs the counsellor to provide or supplement from her own resources in a concrete way. This is, of course, consistent with the situation's face-value: the client, simply by becoming a client, indicates that he is not functioning well enough and requires help. The circumstances are often urgent, particularly with adolescents – something must be done quickly to alter or resolve the situation. By responding to that pressure, the counsellor implicitly defines 'help' as removing distress or anxiety as soon as possible. In doing so, she may also satisfy her need to be helpful and gratifying.

Ivan Illich in *Medical Nemesis* (1975) makes the point that our social structure rests on the double premise that individuals have the right *not* to suffer and that they need not bear responsibility for themselves and their actions. The combination of social welfare and extensive specialization fosters dependence, irresponsibility and unrealistic expectations about what is due to us as citizens. We have experts in almost every area of personal and domestic functioning – people to bake our bread, build our houses, defend us against allegations, protect our money, cure us of disease. Experts are obviously useful: they are efficient and they free us to do other things, but we are so accustomed to them that we only intermittently question whether we need be so reliant on them, and indeed we often expect them to provide for us as a natural right. (In a bread strike, for instance, it was asserted that we have an inalienable right to bread. Apparently that right extends to having the bread *provided* for us.) The slogan for a credit card 'Take the waiting out of wanting' catches Illich's meaning, but he deplores what the advertisers encourage.

Counsellors are experts and are not exempt from these expectations. Clients do want something that will put an end to their need just as a trip to the doctor meets their need for relief from physical distress. The problem, however, is that so long as one individual wants or needs the goods provided by another and cannot imagine that he could provide them for himself, he is tied into that relationship and is forced to perpetuate it. Dynamically, he has projected the helping part of himself into the counsellor and therefore has to stay with her, in order to stay in contact with that part of himself. The counsellor's responsibility is not to make herself indispensable in that way; her ultimate aim is to make herself redundant for that client. Active intervention on behalf of the client who believes that this is his due, and who has no confidence in, and no evidence of, his own resources, only increases his dependence and intensifies his sense of helplessness. He may have been helped through that particular difficulty, but he had been deprived of an opportunity for growth, a chance to conceptualize, generalize and discover how to use his abilities in the future to manage the next difficulty more effectively or even to avoid it altogether. Nor has he helped himself to tolerate frustration, either with the world or with his own imperfection, which is the cardinal and perhaps most painful adjustment we ever have to make.

Counsellors need not deprecate their expertise, but they can more profitably purvey a process than a product: the purpose of counselling is to enable the client to help himself: helping him is not sufficient. As well as understanding his circumstances, a counsellor provides the client with a model for understanding and managing himself, and in the long run this is more valuable because it allows the client to become autonomous. Clearly with young people this is complicated because they are in the midst of the attempt to work out their own dependence-independence balance. They are struggling to learn to live with the consequences of their actions and decisions. Permitting them to evade this conflict by taking over the initiative does not allow them to resolve it, and, perhaps more essential, it deprives them of feeling good and having the credit when things go well. It's like the intrusive, too-good mother who pre-empts the child's experience by knowing too much or acting too soon.

Ted, who had been too disturbed to work for several years, was at last ready to work again. Not surprisingly, he had difficulty getting the sort of job he wanted. His counsellor also wanted him to be working and was anxious lest the demoralizing interviews set him back. Having contacts in his field of interest, she offered direct help. Ted was furious and felt insulted. He read into the offer her lack of confidence in his ability to struggle through this difficult phase and her belief that his own resources weren't good enough. He was quite right, of course. Wanting to stem her own anxiety, she had lost sight of the fact that the most useful help was to bear with him in the slow and painful process of social reintegration, just as she had through his personal integration.

Or, as another client put it, while discussing his tendency to set up utterly dependent relationships and his phantasy of clinging helplessly to his counsellor: 'But I know people swallowed whole give me indigestion.'

The extension from intervening directly to using oneself explicitly as a model for the client is simple and obvious, and the consequences are similar. It is, of course, impossible to disregard personal experience, and it will influence one's work extensively and subtly. However, an intervention that begins, silently or aloud, as 'If it were me ...' risks a failure to distinguish between me and him and is an invitation for him to try to be like me as I am or ought to be. Neither is a step in the direction of autonomy for the client, and both are likely to generate depression or envy, which will not help the client to evaluate himself realistically. Furthermore, there is patently no reason to assume that counsellors are the best models, nor that what is good for one person is necessarily good for the next. What will be 'good' is each person's ability to appraise his own situation and from there discover how things could be different.

Turning now to the other end of the continuum, the non-directive stance. Here the basic assumption is that the client does have the resources for making decisions and sorting out his relationships, but he is prevented from moving or changing because of unresolved anxieties. Help comes through talking about himself in a broad and historical way, during which the anxieties and defences will become evident and will be worked through in the transference, thus clearing the way for the client to act effectively. The mood of the sessions is reflective and help is likely to take time and involve pain and stress. For clients who are up against some real or emotional deadline, this approach runs the risk of not respecting their immediate difficulties. If already feeling shamefully inadequate, and faced by the silent and remote counsellor who is apparently so unhelpful and so vastly different from what he expected, the client can feel overwhelmed by a sense of helplessness and isolation and may retreat into depression or angry, spurious independence. While the directive approach invites dependence based on gratification and denial of independence, the non-directive stance invites an equally binding tie where the counsellor's power lies in withholding and mystification. The client stays in the hope of someday getting both what he came for and the counsellor's 'magic'.

INTERFERING AND INTERVENING

Counsellors, no less than anyone else, have to live with the consequences of their behaviour and decisions. Offering a decision or an opinion opens them up to guilt, gratification and the possibility of being misused and misconstrued because of the transference distortions which creep in. On the other hand, refraining from active and direct intervention leaves them at the mercy of anxiety about what decisions and actions the client will take. Seeing him move in directions which arouse uneasiness or disapproval raises serious moral and ethical questions about the nature of responsibility: conflict between the belief that he should arrive at his own resolutions and the intention to prevent him from harming himself further is often intolerable, and leads to action sooner rather than later out of fear of being burdened with guilt if things go drastically wrong. Often, however, there is no need to act at all. An episode in the work with Eleanor is a salutary tale.

Eleanor was an only child, brought up in a restrictive and suspicious household consisting of herself, her mother and grandmother (who was actually dead but lived on as a strong presence). Her father had deserted before Eleanor was born, and she and her mother lived in a very close bond which had hatred of men as a fundamental part of its 'glue'. When her mother died, Eleanor felt life was pointless, grew suicidal and came for counselling. The sessions were painful, so she was doubly glad to be snatched from her misery by Sam, an older man who consoled her with stories of his loss of wife and child and offered her an exciting relationship – although she was overawed by his claimed connections with parliament, the aristocracy and the police. Within weeks they were talking about marriage, and he was using huge sums of her inherited money to set up a business. Much about Sam seemed implausible to the counsellor, and the decision to marry seemed to be made on entirely the wrong basis. Even Eleanor saw that the relationship and their plans caused her more anxiety than pleasure, but so great was her need for a close twosome based on shared misery and her fear of being on her own, that she could ignore all she saw and felt.

When Sam had a 'heart attack' Eleanor called in her own doctor who diagnosed it as a psychosomatic stress reaction. This doctor had originally referred her for counselling, and the counsellor had shared her concern with him over time, so he used this opportunity to check Sam's medical record. He discovered a long list of psychiatric admissions and prison sentences, all for exploitation and confidence tricks. He urged the counsellor to reveal all, but she refused and dissuaded him from doing so on the basis of her feeling that Eleanor would simply refuse to believe it. By now the marriage was imminent. Eleanor had perceived that the counsellor opposed the marriage but angrily interpreted that as the counsellor's jealousy and man-hatred. She rejected all concern as being just like her mother's attempts to prevent her having boyfriends. Since her mother's theme had been that men exploit women, any attempt to use the information about Sam would have been doomed to feed further the strong negative transference.

Sam failed to keep a follow-up appointment with the doctor, but Eleanor appeared in his place. As they discussed her plans, the doctor expressed his surprise that she knew so few facts about her future husband. She began a search, and did it with such thoroughness that Sam ended up in court again. The experience was devastating for her, but she was adamant that any direct interference by doctor or counsellor would simply have made her more determined to marry this man. These were harrowing weeks during which the counsellor had to bear her anxiety about apparently condoning a disastrous future for Eleanor, the doctor's sceptical disapproval, and Eleanor's blatant irrationality. Although Eleanor was helplessly caught up in self-destructiveness there would have been no point in simply telling her that; she had to find it out through her own experience in order for it to mean anything.

It would, of course, have been impossible for the counsellor to conceal her serious misgivings about Eleanor's relationship with Sam. As much as counsellors try to remain impartial and neutral, a 'blank screen' is patently impossible since all personal feelings and opinions simply cannot be edited out. Conscious control and containment are only partially successful, and the counsellor's own unconscious remains to be reckoned with. Keeping personal reactions out of the counselling relationship is perhaps most difficult when deeply held beliefs and attitudes are called into play, and even more troublesome when the counsellor suspects that her beliefs are not entirely rational. Religious and political ideas, attitudes towards sexuality, and concepts about personal success and failure and good relationships are huge areas of vulnerability, but so are apparently lesser matters like smoking, dress and appearance. One counsellor who held toiletries in contempt found it impossible to take seriously her client's distress over his stolen deodorant. Uncertainty about the validity of their beliefs can make counsellors avoid a particular area or turn it into an arena for debate so that the client is not helped to understand the significance of that belief for him.

> Ian had experienced a problematic religious conversion and frequently blocked exploration of his behaviour with the statement 'because God says so'. While understanding some of the dynamics of conversion in the life of such a lonely and frightened man the counsellor felt that her own religious scepticism was riddled with irrational feelings and so avoided the topic. Instead she left the sessions feeling very sorry for God who seemed powerless to stop such degrading abuse of Himself.

Strongly held religious, political and philosophical beliefs can give a client, particularly a young person, both relief and distress. Unless they can understand their beliefs as reflections of their inner state, they cannot begin to resolve their problems, and to do that they need a counsellor who is sure of her own ground, but won't impose her beliefs on them.

Clients frequently perceive the counsellor's refusal to intervene or to offer herself as yardstick as uncaring and irresponsible - a descendant of Pontius Pilate, who stands aside and lets unruly forces take their toll. This is so particularly if the client has a vested interest in maintaining his dependence and irresponsibility. The examples just given should make it clear that she holds back so that the client may have time and space to discover and develop his own resources and controls. Counsellors are, none the less, constantly attempting to be influential in the lives of their client, but they try to keep a clear distinction between personal and professional influence.

The initial contact with a client usually contains a statement to the effect that the time allocated is his and he is free to use that time as he chooses. Such a statement is only partially true: it is his time in the sense of being protected as well as possible against intrusions and the counsellor will not use it for herself, but she will retain the right to influence the interaction toward more productive work. It is a commonplace that clients often present initially with a problem masking their real difficulty, and the counsellor will redirect the focus as the underlying problem becomes evident. Regardless of how well motivated the client is, he is likely to defend himself, consciously or unconsciously, against pain, and it is the counsellor's responsibility within the work contract not to collude with that avoidance: she repeatedly returns to the distressing area at a pace the client can tolerate.

Penny presented with acute examination anxiety. There was no doubt that she was in a panic and was wearing herself out with an inefficient study programme. The matter was urgent because exams were imminent, but formulating a better study plan did not relieve her problem. She would talk only about the exams, but two aspects were noteworthy: she could not conceive of life after her finals, and had avoided, almost phobically, planning ahead; and she had a dread of getting a second-class degree which would, in her view, fix her for ever as a second-class citizen. The counsellor wondered where that idea came from and in an unguarded response Penny stated angrily that she would not be like her mother. She regretted that outburst because it made her think about her family situation – her father had repeatedly left home, leaving his wife and children to fare as best they might. She was the 'clever' one and, with a degree, was likely also to be abandoning her family for a different world. Her boyfriend was planning to move, leaving her to choose whether she followed him or not. But she didn't want to talk about relationships ('it's bad to stir up feelings') although they were clearly relevant to her anxiety. She grudgingly admitted feeling better when she could sort out her feelings about herself, her parents and her boyfriend, but she had to be pushed to it and was relieved to escape at the end of term.

For Penny, her exam anxiety was acutely distressing, but it was paradoxically very safe. She gave a repeat performance every year, secure in the knowledge that she would do well, and her flamboyant panic could distract her from the far more upsetting relationship and identity difficulties inevitably aroused at exam time. Clients who use one problem as a defence against another approach counselling with intense ambivalence, hoping on the one hand to deceive and be left in peace, and on the other to be helped to face the underlying problem. A counsellor who avoids a difficult area of experience or feeling does a double disservice to her client. Failing to tackle a significant aspect is a kind of deprivation: and colluding with avoidance may make the client feel that such feelings can't be handled, thereby reinforcing anxiety and diminishing any optimism about using those feelings constructively.

Like Penny, Brian's presenting problem was not his real preoccupation but, unlike her, he readily tackled it. First, however, he was in danger of hasty action and needed help to see the consequences of his intentions.

Brian had just failed an important oral exam in his post-graduate programme. His two contemporaries, both supervised by the professor, had passed. He was convinced he knew more than they did, accused the examiners of favouritism and being afraid to fail the professor's students, and intended to lodge a formal complaint with the authorities. The notion of publicly disgracing the examiners delighted him. Although he had the letter of complaint in his pocket, the fact that he dropped into the counsellor's office to ask to whom he should deliver it belied his intentions and provided a starting-point for discussion. By the end of the meeting he readily acknowledged his own humiliation at failing, and his own anxiety about his poor standard of work due to personal upsets during the year - feelings he would prefer someone else to have. However, he decided that his plans were likely to further disgrace him, rather than his examiners, and there were more effective and less defensively hostile means of getting a reassessment of his work.

By helping clients think through a decision counsellors will not always protect them from hurtful experiences, but they do convey a willingness to stand by them when they are bruised. There is never room for saying 'I told you so'; moralizing is always a deterrent to understanding.

LIFE-AND-DEATH MATTERS

When a client's or another's life or well-being is at stake, the counsellor may need to intervene more intensively. Here, as in everything else, however, she needs to be quick-witted rather than hastily active. Suicide is probably the nightmare of all counsellors, not least because those who seriously intend to kill themselves do not always openly make the threat, and indeed may carefully conceal their plans from everyone. Those who do threaten suicide create uncertainty about whether they really mean it or whether they are trying to elicit attention, or promote guilt or fear in the counsellor. A counsellor's first sources of support – access to a competent colleague for a second opinion, and ready knowledge of the local hospital admission and emergency procedures, if not actual stand-by arrangements – should already exist as part of her professional network, to be used if necessary. With the client it may be appropriate to offer more time and to seek his co-operation in establishing a protective network for him, but more time and greater vigilance is no substitute for getting at the feelings behind the suicidal impulse.

Put simply, suicidal wishes reflect either a tremendous sense of alienation, or an unmanageable anger mixed with revenge. In the first instance, existential isolation, clues to the seriousness of the threat lie in knowing whether there is anyone to whom the client feels attached in the most fundamental sense. Within the relationship this means looking at the resilience of the therapeutic alliance. It is not enough that there is 'someone or something to live for', and trying to persuade the client that there is, when there isn't, is futile. In the second case, clues lie in discovering whether the client feels unbearably guilty about his anger (probably unconscious) with someone, past, present or counsellor, and has turned the attack against himself. Along with the characteristic depression of this internal state, there is usually a sadistic (and gleeful) component by which the client would have someone else feel guilty or afraid. The frequently expressed sense of worthlessness can refer to both routes to suicide – of having been abandoned to his terrors or being irredeemably 'bad'. It is not time for pussy-footing: the aliena- tion, terrors, anger, guilt and sadistic wishes need to be confronted robustly and directly. Suicide, after all, requires courage, so the client is not entirely fragile and can stand it; he is more likely to feel frightened and insecure if he perceives fear or hostility in the coun- sellor. If the counsellor reacts by feeling paralysed with helplessness, it's probable that these feelings are being projected by the client, who feels impotent to deal with himself constructively although it should be remembered that her power in the situation is realistically limited since the final decision lies with the client.

When someone or something else is endangered, an attempt must first be made to work directly with the client on the motives and conse- quences of his intentions. If he can mobilize his concern and guilt (from the 'sometimes' phase or 'depressive position'); can reassert internal control over his harmful impulses, and truly own them as his (part of him rather than a threat to him as they surely would be if he acted on them); and can understand the symbolic place of the action in his internal world, then the danger is likely to pass. If not, then the coun- sellor has little choice but to tell him that she will inform relevant people and have him constrained. Internal control is always more effective than external restraint, it leaves the client less angry and frightened or punished by his own wishes; but this control occurs at a profound level. Verbal assurances must be backed up by appropriate feelings of remorse for the counsellor to accept them. In these situa- tions, as in suicide, feelings must be dealt with firmly but without hostility, and the client's power to frighten and damage himself, her or others has to be clearly acknowledged. Imagined or threatened destruc- tion will always be survived, but actual attack may not be. In these major matters, when a client clearly hasn't the ego-strength to prevent himself from acting out his phantasies in reality, the counsellor steps in temporarily and only as an alternative and covering ego (remembering that Winnicott said a baby's ego is as good as his mother's ego- support), never as a punitive superego.

Fortunately these kinds of crisis are relatively rare, but counselling is undoubtedly stressful and demanding for the counsellor, and she owes it to herself and her clients to protect herself and to safeguard the work against gratuitous stress. If she is tired, rushed, distracted, intruded upon, uncertain of her own position and skill, and too prone to carry away the feelings and worries of her clients, then she cannot work effectively and competently, and the clients will suffer. This basic responsibility of self-protection is fulfilled through organizing the working-place and day, being clear about her motives in doing the work, and acquiring adequate professional support.

MANAGING THE WORK

It may seem trivial or officious to insist upon a quiet and sound-proof room, comfortable chairs, a telephone bell that can be turned off, and anything else contributing to a calm and relaxed atmosphere, but such things are as fundamental to the work as a microscope is to a biologist. Clients can seldom feel secure enough to get on with their work if the counsellor herself doesn't feel at home, is subject to interruptions, or is always having to be prepared to defend her territory. Uncertainty about privacy and sovereignty is contagious to the client, and an unsettled counsellor obviously cannot give the undivided attention and concentration she implicitly offers. Establishing a right to proper facilities is a legitimate part of the counsellor's work; obtaining them is a sign of recognition of her authority.

The 'fifty-minute hour' usually elicits a sceptical smile about the ritual and rigmarole of the therapeutic business along with the couch and the pounce on a Freudian slip. The actual truncated hour is not sacred, but the underlying principle of building in time for reflection on the session is. Especially if several clients are seen consecutively, but even with a single client, a space for both consolidating and distancing from an interview is necessary. Remembering is a physiological process which happens automatically if given time; useful remembering requires concentration and effort. 'Rerunning' a session, noting its themes, moods, information and questions makes it more available for recall at the next meetings; grasping it as a whole helps to place it in the sequence of sessions. If the counsellor can establish the client's continuity in her own mind and can see broader themes, developments and change through weeks of work, she can both offer the client a perception of himself and alert herself more effectively to important aspects of the work. (The problem of keeping records of the sessions arises here. Some people find the act of writing itself an aid to memory; others find that putting the material on paper usurps memory and leaves a great void in their heads. Some need an almost verbatim account for it to be meaningful; others can use only cryptic phrases which have none the less caught the gist and atmosphere of the session for them. It is a matter of personal style and efficiency.) The time after a session is usually not tranquil. Clients will say that sometimes it takes days to recover from a session, and they often do some very useful emotional work in the aftermath. Counsellors also have to recover and can use the time and the remaining feelings to reflect on what has just happened. Sometimes new themes emerge, or small details which had been submerged in the pursuit of another theme stand out as vitally important. Any session can usually be 'read' in a number of ways, and this 'ego work' of thinking and rethinking it, reordering hypotheses, linking it with the past, and storing it, is no less important than the work done in the session itself. Rushing off to do something else which requires attention interferes with the ego work. This immediate consolidation, of course, needs to be followed up with reflection at a greater distance later, and there should be time to go through the mental or written notes immediately before seeing the client again as a form of preparation.

Ego work also enables the counsellor to disengage from a session: it stops the momentum of the interview, deals with her feelings aroused by it, and gets it out of her system so she is emotionally free for the next client. It will be evident by now that feelings respect no boundaries, even in counsellors, and it is all too easy to confuse clients - relating to one with feelings pertinent to the last; even saying to one a delayed response to the last.

A time space between clients is a physical aid to the psychological process of keeping firm boundaries, but it also eases time boundaries. Many clients leave the most important bits for last, and although sessions cannot be substantially prolonged in collusion with the client, some leeway in the time at least avoids cutting them off in midstream and gives the counsellor a chance to comment on the tactic itself. Time boundaries are a feature of professional consistency, and it is important to begin and end meetings promptly, but some flexibility relieves the counsellor of having to be an anxious and surreptitious clock-watcher. She is then free to concentrate on the vital first and last minutes of the session.

At a dynamic level, all clients will probably be involved in some form of rivalry for love and attention. Jealousy, competition and the associated feelings of losing and winning favour will enter into the counselling relationships, and these need not be unnecessarily provoked by the counsellor setting up a situation where clients pass each other on the way in or out, or where one is kept waiting while another gets extra time and care. Equally unnecessary is exposing clients to a harassed or tired counsellor who, like the Old Woman who lived in a shoe, has so many clients she doesn't know what to do. Human emotional resources and memory are finite; only a limited number of clients can be worked with at any point in time. The size of a manageable workload is personal - counsellors vary in the number of life histories they can recall and keep distinct, and in the amount of transference and emotional stress they can manage. Characteristics of different phases of work, however, influence the amount of emotional and intellectual energy required. The initial phase of contact, when the counsellor needs to familiarize herself with the life-story and style of a new client, is demanding; and the final phase of termination, with the inevitable sense of loss and regret, is emotionally taxing. Planned focal work requires a discipline and concentration absent from long-term 'follow the material' work. With long-term clients there are plateaux which need special effort to overcome. The nature of the work obviously does not allow clients to be picked up and put down in juggling toward a realistic workload, so some extra space needs to be left vacant for these peak periods or for the predictable unexpected crisis. Demands on counsellors are often far greater than they can meet. It is difficult to refuse someone in need of help, but to take on another client without the necessary time and emotional energy is counter-productive and spuriously helpful. Denying the need for a rest and time (including taking sensible breaks from work altogether) may be falling into the trap of feeling omnipotent and indispensable. Clients are often over-ready to feel anxious and guilty about the demands they make on their counsellors, and it is unkind and unprofessional to exacerbate those feelings by irresponsible planning.

MANAGING MOTIVES

Having the discipline and confidence to structure the physical conditions of work can be difficult, but organizing motives and feelings within the work is often more taxing, and more central to being responsible in the work. Many people believe that counselling is simply a matter of common sense and can be done by anyone who is level-headed and good-hearted. It attracts people seeking an outlet for their need to be helpful and socially useful. A level head, good heart and an inclination to help and understand people may be necessary, but they are certainly not sufficient. If these are all the counsellor has to offer, the clients, not content with being gratifyingly understood, will rapidly exhaust her resources and lead her out of her intellectual and emotional depth. The consequent anxiety, and sometimes resentment, aroused in the counsellor can block the relationship and force her to blunder on to some kind of resolution – usually termination or referral.

> Tim worked in a youth club and, because the youngsters trusted him with their problems, was beginning to think of himself as a counsellor. He had managed to establish a good relationship with one of the girls who frequented the club and was generally avoided by others because she was temperamental and had an alarming history of suicide attempts. She came from a chaotic and deprived family, and Tim understood that her behaviour was largely attention-seeking. In time she became very attached to him and began to resent his spending time with others or on his work. During a busy period she began to threaten suicide again – a manoeuvre which Tim saw as a protest about his busyness, but he felt he couldn't cope with that on top of everything else, so he virtually ignored her. She did take an overdose, went through the hospital routine, and was discharged without help or support and with the punishment of being told she was a nuisance yet again. Tim was angry with the hospital and still felt inadequate to the problem when she sought him out again. The hours he spent trying to refer her for 'proper counselling' – unsuccessfully – could have been used far more effectively working directly with the girl. Intuitively Tim understood her need for a special and dependable relationship, but his fear that she would drain him made him avoid her and that drove her deeper into 'suicide'. With training and supervision to support him, he met with her regularly and the threats diminished dramatically.

Counsellors need not only to recognize that clients are in distress; they also need to know how and why they are in distress in order to choose and pursue an appropriate therapeutic strategy which will neither avoid nor perpetuate the client's problem. This requires training - the acquisition of a theoretical framework and a full understanding of the nature of the counselling relationship - preferably through being on the receiving end of counselling as well as through study. That is a hard intellectual and emotional job. It is disturbing and ironic that the staunchest supporters of the 'kindness and natural ability' counselling (the ones who avoid training, and reject theories as impersonal and denigrating) are often more concerned with their own well-being than with the client's and are looking for a relatively painless way of assuring themselves that they are good people. If they do get involved more than superficially, they soon find themselves in a very painful world indeed.

It is a commonplace to assume that all people in the helping professions are attempting to sort out some personal problem by pursuing this particular kind of work, and this is probably so. An interest in people, a sensitive perceptiveness about others, and a readiness to understand and explain human behaviour, all may be subtle ways of soothing personal anxieties, feeling slightly removed by being in the observer's seat, using the understanding to see where one stands in relation to others, experiencing a sense of control. These can all be servants to the counselling process, but if they become paramount they over-burden and distort the work so neither party is satisfied or helped.

Amy was completing a probationary year as an untrained social worker. Her caseload had reached the usual inhuman level, and she was feeling immobilized by the amount of work and the apparent lack of results for all her effort. A supervisor had sustained her throughout the year by offering some counselling within the supervision, but now he gave her less time and hinted that she needed a lot of help. She consulted a counsellor to decide whether she should continue as a social worker at all. Amy's entire family was in trouble. Her father was chronically ill and bad-tempered and proudly rejected any care. Mother had fled from him into an affair, one sister was anorexic and the other depressed. Amy was the 'strong one', managing to deny her needs in order to meet and survive the family demands and tensions. Urged on by unconscious guilt at having escaped obvious illness but not having helped her family, she drifted through sociology to social work. The clients continued to arouse her guilt, and in the supervisor she found a man prepared to notice her needs, but only so long as they were apparently work-related. This illusion suited her since the myth was that she had no personal needs. By surreptitiously meeting her needs, however, he undermined this myth, and his withdrawal brought her to crisis point: her denial of her needy self and the experience of a caring 'father' were simultaneously destroyed.

She found it difficult to be a client herself and tried to set up a colleague-to-colleague dialogue. She was apologetic for using time when there were so many other desperately needy people around. She understood her family's problems and rehearsed them like a catechism, but she couldn't connect them emotionally with herself. Interpretations about her anxieties and defences humiliated and angered her because she experienced them as accusations of inadequacy and weakness. She subscribed to the familiar double standard that problems in a client are 'normal' and help-worthy, but problems in the helper are bad and unacceptable. Before she could be helped, she needed to respect her own needs and to have compassion rather than hatred for her imperfections. When she could do this, she discovered that some of the problems she had imagined to be in her clients were her own projected on to them, and by working simultaneously with herself and with her clients, she found her work far less dispiriting and the clients less intractable.

Unless the 'helpers' see when they are unconsciously trying to help themselves by trying to resolve their own distress embodied in the client, frustration and depression set in. Whether or not the client 'gets better', the needy and disturbed part of the counsellor becomes overt and clamours for direct attention. A vicious spiral develops as the counsellor becomes less able to cope with the work and erects a formidable set of defences against failure which interfere with attempts to both give and receive help.

Even very experienced counsellors will have their work upset by their personal needs and anxieties from time to time, so training and therapy for themselves is no absolute guarantee against such difficult phases. The difference between the responsible and irresponsible counsellor is that the first knows what is likely to happen, cares enough about the client to monitor herself for areas and moments of vulnerability, and has the courage and humility to confront her needs and anxieties, while the second is too arrogant or too scared to see such potential within herself. It seems paradoxical that those who profess to care selflessly about others often care least and suffer most because of their deception, while those who selfishly set aside time and energy to look to, and after, themselves show true concern for others and find genuine satisfaction in their work.

Training is a large subject in its own right and is outside the scope of this book. However, training should provide counsellors with a sense of what they can do and the confidence to do it; an awareness of their weak and blind spots and the discretion not to tumble helplessly into them with clients; and a theoretical framework to support them. Training never ends, but usually continues through supervision, where both personal and professional matters, as they relate to work with clients, are discussed. The most effective and appropriate training, however, is personal therapy or counselling. Nowhere else is there the opportunity to focus on personal dynamics, feelings and intentions. The counsellor's own emotional resources are her greatest ally in her work, so if she is ignorant of them, afraid of them, or unable to rely on them, she is severely handicapped – and she handicaps her clients. In a simple piece of research, one counsellor found that his colleagues who had been trained felt more competent in their work, commanded more respect in their workplace, and consequently felt yet more confident. Untrained counsellors felt they had to rely entirely on personal regard for their reputation and self-esteem. A counsellor's authority, her right to practise and to have the confidence of clients and colleagues, ultimately rests on her skills and her integrity.

7 ‖ Counselling in organizations

All counsellors work within some kind of organizational structure and will be influenced by it to the extent that it is immediately visible and formally ordered. Paradoxically those who share the physical premises with their clients and colleagues from other disciplines are most likely to feel that they are separate and work in isolation. Even if she is the only counsellor around, this sense of being alone is commonly a consequence of confusion arising from inadequately defined work objectives and a failure to understand the dynamics of institutional relationships. All too frequently counsellors concentrate on improving their understanding of individuals and the therapeutic relationship at the expense of comprehending the context in which they (the counsellors) live and work. However, it is now generally recognized that simply belonging to an organization can create stress, and malfunctioning in an organization can generate personal problems in all its members and seriously impair its productivity. Conversely, a malfunctioning individual can severely disrupt the work of an organization. Counsellors will profit from understanding the conscious and unconscious dynamics of their work environment, if only by appreciating the nature of the stresses and constraints they experience in trying to do their work. Furthermore, it puts them in a better position to participate in and influence decisions concerning the welfare of the organization as a whole.

Organizations, like individuals, operate at more than one level simultaneously. There is usually a set of formal roles, tasks and systems of accountability established for the pursuit of the conscious goals of the enterprise, but there is also a set of informal and personal roles and relationships, emotional tasks and unconscious dynamics which may help or hinder the achievement of those goals. (It has been said, for instance, that certain companies exist ostensibly to make and sell cars, but from time to time it appears that their primary task is to keep people employed – an objective pursued at the expense of the stated aim.) Individual members will go to work and return home after performing certain tasks every day, but they will also arrive eagerly or apprehensively and leave stimulated or harassed after a series of inter-personal encounters and moments of anxiety, exasperation, satisfaction or pleasure, depending on whether they have been able to do or be what they are personally there for, and whether their goals are the same as the organization's. Because they are so complex, and because of discrepancies between conscious and unconscious intentions, both individually and organizationally, organizations are fertile grounds for confusion, misunderstanding, phantasies and frustration.

For counsellors, most difficulties arise because the nature of their work is poorly understood by others, and it is often felt to be at variance with the objectives of others. In an educational institution, for example, where the primary emphasis is on intellectual achievement, the vagaries of emotional development may be a virtual mystery to many academics and administrators, and recognition of the need of some members to spend time sorting out personal problems is apparently inconsistent with the college's need to maintain high academic standards. These difficulties are exacerbated when counsellors cannot or do not define and explain their work sufficiently to others (or even to themselves), and when they have neglected to tackle whatever internal uncertainties and conflicts they (as members of the organization) may have over objectives.

ROLES AND TASKS

Each member of an organization has a specified role and task which are defined or described in terms of expectations or limitations of activity and which, in turn, are intended to facilitate the purpose of the organization. Having joined, an individual is seldom free to act in a personal capacity – he now has to act in the interests of that organization, even becoming the personification of its function and being seen by others as representing it. This obviously imposes a number of constraints and stresses. Like the medieval man, he is subject to external pressures and demands, and he allows himself to be shaped by these so he may be an acceptable and useful member. Consequently he may have to restrain some of his personal qualities and forgo preferred kinds of behaviour while developing other capabilities which he doesn't have or isn't comfortable with simply in order to fulfil the organization's expectations and needs. However, like the Renaissance man, he wants to express and achieve his own needs, ideals and capabilities and so may exert counter-pressures to redefine his role and influence his environment toward greater personal satisfaction. When there is a substantial discrepancy between his needs to be both accepted and individually expressive and between the behaviours associated with those needs, and when organizational objectives and personal or professional integrity and aspirations differ significantly, then personal and institutional conflicts ensue, as these two examples show.

> Miss J. belonged to a counselling organization which had strict guidelines for how counsellors should respond to clients. She understood that the rules existed to protect both parties, but she also felt the rules were based on the assumptions that all counsellors had the same degree of expertise and that all clients required a merely sympathetic response. She soon grew frustrated and felt her skills were under-used. If she observed the rules, the contact was non-productive for some clients and unsatisfying to herself; if she used her initiative, she feared becoming unacceptable herself – a fear partially confirmed by an attempt at discussion with her superior, who simply re-explained the rules for her. Since organizational change was impossible, she then began to have a daily debate with herself about whether or not to go to work and stay with the service; whether the satisfaction she did have in work there offset the frustrations and misgivings.

> Mr R. worked as a student services officer in a college which generally treated its welfare staff as an outpost of the main organization. Having no formal access to decision-making committees he wrote a memo to the Principal setting out the probable undesirable consequences for students of a proposed regulation currently under discussion. The Principal responded by reminding him curtly that his job was to deal with problems presented by the students *when* they happened; his views were not required by a committee capable of thinking for itself.

In both these cases, the roles were unusually limited, but at least in Miss J.'s case the job requirements were painstakingly explicit and fixed, so she was left with a personal dilemma. Mr R., on the other hand, had frequent cause to repent his optimism when accepting the job. There had been no job description on the grounds that 'We all know what you counsellor types do.' He had thought this would give him unlimited scope for activity, but instead the mutual avoidance of any terms of reference meant that he so often unwittingly offended the unspoken norms that his sphere of activity was regularly restricted incident by incident, and it became impossible to establish reasonable role and task definitions. In the end, he resorted to a kind of guerrilla warfare within the college and vacillated between triumph and apprehension.

In two further examples, the counsellors also did less than they could and wanted to, not because they were organizationally limited but because they were not secure and explicit about the skills and authority they possessed. Both experienced a combination of personal and organizational turmoil.

Miss L. was creating a counselling role in a small school and felt undervalued by the director who tended to ignore her and her comments about the state of the school. After two years of dissatisfying work, she took stock and realized two vital points: she had never stated her skills positively and had deliberately kept a low profile to avoid anticipated attack. So the director, who had never worked with a counsellor before, didn't know what she could do or how to use her assertively. This director also was uncomfortable about having women colleagues and Miss L. had responded to this by being 'typically' feminine – either so emotional that she threatened his reserve, or tentatively submissive, thus losing sight of her genuine professionalism.

Mrs F. had worked for several years in a dual role which had teaching and counselling components. She had mixed feelings when that job was disbanded and she was offered a full-time counselling post. She found that she was too self-conscious in this more defined role to relate to clients naturally, and she couldn't cope with the resentment and expectations of the other already established welfare staff. She hid guiltily and anxiously in her office, creating unnecessary paperwork. Change is always unsettling, but Mrs F. seemed to have left her skills behind with the lost job and consequently couldn't discuss them and her role in relation to her new colleagues.

These four examples indicate that the overt conflict between individual and organization usually occurs over performance in the job, and so it would seem possible to resolve differences if the individual simply performed differently. However, because behaviour reflects personality, such change is difficult. Even if behavioural change is forced by circumstance, the internal inconsistency may be ultimately intolerable. Miss L. and Mrs F., for instance, were both quiet women, both uneasy about their own aggression, and so it was extremely stressful for them to manufacture the assertive behaviour required of them. On the other hand, Miss J. was a decisive young woman who had made her way in the world single-handed, and Mr R. was defiant and rebellious, so for both of them the need to submit to a large system was at one level simply unacceptable. Sometimes, of course, it works the opposite way: an individual may have the necessary qualities for performing the work but is perceived as unpleasant to others in the organization. In one counselling organization, the scrupulous finance officer was unpopular but grudgingly respected because he resisted all appeals to the heart-strings, keeping a firm and realistic hand on the purse-strings.

The link between personality and behaviour is also evident when individuals take up emotional roles within the work setting. Because groups and institutions have an emotional life as well as a rational existence, alongside the prescribed, consciously delegated, task-based roles and activities runs a parallel but less orderly system of unconsciously allocated emotional roles and activities. Just as individuals will respond to achievement, failure and frustration in their work, so will groups as whole units. When the work is going badly, when objectives are unclear, and when overt or covert strife between members breaks out, energy and concentration is diverted away from the rational work of the organization to the emotional business of individual and corporate survival.

WORKING AND SURVIVING IN GROUPS

Bion (1961) developed this concept of survival in groups. He observed that there is always a struggle to keep at the work-task in the face of anxieties about competition, envy, failure and frustration. When these threaten group cohesion, it takes refuge in activities which may look like work, but are actually defensive manoeuvres designed to allay the anxieties and hence automatically avoid the real work. He describes three major patterns of survival behaviour, each reflecting a primitive relationship and each containing a specific assumption about how the group can be rescued from disintegration. The first sort is dependence on an omnipotent and omniscient leader. The leader is selected by the group (or sets himself up and is accepted by the others) and all capabilities are vested in him, leaving the rest passive and helpless yet hopeful. He has all the bright ideas, the right answers, the workable plan. Such a relationship is, of course, unrealistic, and the leader is eventually attacked and sacrificed by the disappointed, enraged or envious members. The fate of the Messiah is crucifixion; that is the archetype for this basic assumption relationship. A second survival stratagem is based on the belief that two people can get together and create a solution for the group, rather like sexual intercourse producing a child upon whom all hopes are pinned. Such couples and 'brain children' are seldom able to meet the heavy expectations placed on them, and they inevitably fail. Furthermore, others may reject the creative pair, attacking their activity out of a sense of jealousy and exclusion. A third alternative is to flee from the problem altogether, often by finding an external enemy against whom they can unite to fight, or by fighting the task itself. These three kinds of activity generate excitement and emotional commitment, but they don't result in real productivity.

A group doesn't, however, always act in concert in these survival activities. When a number of people work together, the opportunity exists for feelings to be polarized and distributed among the members, so that certain individuals can be selected (or self-selected) to experience and express them. These emotional roles are not fixed and may shift according to circumstances, but there are again recognizable patterns. It may be that a group as a whole is denying a particular feeling about the work, and by the mechanism of projection attributes one individual with the feeling in question, and he becomes unaccountably severely depressed or anxious. In other instances, one individual may be in touch with the feeling denied by others, and any attempt on his part to express it is met with opposition and dismissal. Highly charged arguments may ensue, and in this manner the group attempts to resolve its ambivalence. In a third situation, all may share a feeling, but one person is selected to carry it on behalf of the others who retain their equanimity with the result that his behaviour is seen as understandable but unreasonably excessive. In line with all such denial and projection, however, the feeling must fit: the person carrying or expressing the polarized emotion must already have that feeling latent within, or a low threshold for, expressing it.

A group of consultants who had worked together for several years in an advisory capacity to a company had apparently worked themselves out of a job. They had shared their expertise with the company's staff which now felt competent to take over the work and dispense with them. The general tenor of the meeting when the handover was discussed was self-congratulatory elation. Underlying the elation was also some relief since several members of the team had developed in other directions and were ready to leave this particular contract. One member, however, became increasingly depressed during the meeting. She was left to carry the sadness and mourning about ending a fruitful relationship. Her readiness for this role was twofold: she specialized in this kind of training work, and had reservations about the company's ability to do the work effectively, so she would be losing something important and incomplete; and her personal history contained more than a fair share of separations and deaths, so she was sensitized to the pain of loss.

The more enduring personal susceptibilities sometimes cause an individual to become fixed in an emotional role, and he gathers a reputation for always acting in a particular way. What this means is that groups consistently exploit individual predilections for their own purposes.

Miss R. found herself always expressing the anger and frustration in groups. Although she was temperamentally forthright, these outbursts in groups were dramatic and excessive. Recognizing this pattern, when the opportunity arose to work with a group of relative strangers she was determined not to fulfil that particular emotional role. They worked for some time with a noticeable absence of conflict and increasing mediocrity. Another member eventually commented on this, adding that he had expected Miss R. to prod them into sharper interactions. He felt let down by her as now he had to express the nasty frustration. Relieved of being the only angry one, and once the aggression was introduced into the group's work, she could use her assertiveness more naturally, and productive work could be done.

Emotional roles have their counterpart in imagined tasks. This happens when individuals or groups take upon themselves something they haven't been designated to do, and probably can't do because they haven't the requisite resources or authority. This may be at a real level as when, for instance, a group set up to design a project cannot, but nevertheless attempts to, implement it. Failure and criticism usually follow. It also occurs at an unconscious level when the real task gets muddled with a phantasized task. Trainers, for example, are responsible for setting up a training scheme, but they may also unconsciously believe that they are responsible for the trainees' learning. The jocular comment 'We were just solving the problems of the world' expresses the unconsciously accepted task (and hoped-for result) of making everything completely right.

Emotional roles, survival behaviour and imaginary tasks create inefficiency. Business has to be suspended to cope with disproportionate outbursts when the burdened person can no longer contain the projections, and projection automatically means that other members are not functioning fully. Feelings become the enemy of the work rather than facilitators of it. The precious and essential energy is squandered on activities which are doomed to failure both as problem-solvers and anxiety-relievers.

It will be evident by now that whatever the constraints of well-defined roles and tasks, with the expectations and skills clearly spelt out, they are necessary and helpful. Such boundaries function as protective containers which enable work to go on. The individual knows what he is supposed to do, can answer criticisms based on unrealistic or erroneous expectations, and can guard himself and his work against illegitimate encroachment from others. They also provide reference points for distinguishing between the emotional and work roles and between the real and phantasized tasks. The problem for organizations is to achieve the most effective degree of structure for both its members and itself. Too much rigidity inhibits individuality, creativity, and initiative, often leading to a disaffected workforce, and it makes the organization itself ponderous and even resistant to change. Too much flexibility invites anxiety, role confusion, mismanagement, lack of accountability and inadequate professional practice, if not actual motivated chaos.

THE ROLE OF COUNSELLING: REAL AND PHANTASY

Just as individuals can be designated to carry and express particular feelings on behalf of others, whole sections of an organization can be branded with specific attributes not to be found, so it is said, elsewhere in the system. Counselling units are frequently perceived as representing failure, illness and disturbance. When the counsellor's job description and the unit's function are delineated with reference to the organization's overall goals, then the problems surrounding the apparent discrepancy between the aims and business of counselling and the other activities in the organization are considerably eased. This, however, is not often done, usually because the designers of the job are unfamiliar or uncomfortable with the concept of counselling. Even when it is, the given attributes cause it to be shunned and placed at the margin of the organization. This position is appropriate in so far as it is seldom possible or realistic to give a troubled individual the time and attention he needs in the middle of work: there are schedules to keep and other colleagues to consider. Furthermore, probably only a counsellor has the full range of skills to provide effective help. However, when counselling becomes a split-off function, and is effectively placed *outside* the organization, then the arrangement begins to look like an expedient way of putting the disturbance out of sight and mind where it can't cause guilt, distress, anxiety or helplessness in others. When this is the case, counselling really does seem (and indeed can become) a separate and 'deviant' activity. The splitting inevitably leads to untested assumptions which are hard to check since, with less permeable boundaries and less readiness to understand, communication between counsellors and others is made more difficult; opportunities for confusion, misunderstanding and phantasy on both sides are increased. If counsellors don't have easy access to the ordinary working environment of their organization, they have only a partial view of it based on their experience with the troublesome rejects, and others have a similarly skewed view of counselling, associating it almost exclusively with failure and sickness. Each, in the absence of substantial evidence, will 'create' the work of the other according to glimpses, snippets of information, emotionally laden preconceptions and immediate needs. Phantasies, some of them mutually collusive, about counselling occur repeatedly.

A familiar cry among counsellors is that they are used by the institution as a dumping-ground for all the impossible problem people. This does happen, of course. When, in a college, a tutor can no longer understand, manage or tolerate a disturbed student, he may well dispatch the student to the counsellor. Dynamically, this is the equivalent of the harassed mother who tells the difficult child his father will deal with him when he gets home. The worn-out mother feels impotent and so projects all the power onto the father in a rather idealizing, but potentially attacking way. The message is: I trust you will succeed, but I also slightly hope you will fail, so I won't feel inadequate with this culprit, who is intractable. The mothers and tutors are genuinely in need of help and want relief from struggling fruitlessly, but they also feel angry and humiliated by needing help. The counsellor may succeed where the tutor hasn't because she can avoid participating in the built-up frustrating dynamic, but should she also fail, she is in trouble with her own expectations. Counsellors easily fall into the trap of believing that because they set themselves up to help, they must always do so. Faced with not being able to do what she thinks she should do - and unconsciously believes she can do - and finding it difficult to accept failure, she in turn projects the unrealistic demand onto others and feels resentful and helpless. Although complaining that the 'dumpers' are unrealistic, the attribution of being a dumping-ground is met by her unconscious self-perception as a salvage department, transforming and recycling bad and rejected goods into useful products. Only when she has her phantasies under control can she be sure when dumping really is occurring and be in a position to help her colleagues understand her role and capabilities more realistically.

A similar sort of dynamic surrounds the expectation that counsellors will effect remedies at top speed in eleventh-hour crises. This time the phantasy is that she has some magical quality which allows her to defy reality. The referrer is often trying to manage a sense of guilt about not preventing a crisis in someone he has some responsibility for and hopes for alleviation from his colleague. Again, counsellors might like to be able to do the magic and might think they should be able to, but on the whole they can't. The inability to produce a miracle cure often seems to lie behind counsellors' irritation at the disparaging comment that anyone can do what counsellors claim as a special skill; reminders of being human after all offend secret omnipotent wishes.

A different sort of prevalent stereotype is that counsellors are soft and sentimental: they make excuses, plead extenuating circumstances, and demand little of the client. It is true that counsellors tolerate a good deal of malfunctioning and allow the client time and space to arrive at self-understanding and self-motivation. It is also true that counsellors, given access to their history and feelings, readily understand how clients get themselves into irritating, untenable or futile relationships and situations. However, failing to apply pressure and judgements is not necessarily soft; it doesn't inevitably mean letting the client get away with less than he can manage, although it may mean that he does temporarily do less of what is required of him by others. On the contrary, the demands and stress of counselling on the client are often considerable, but the emotional energy is turned inward rather than outward towards the organization's work.

A related myth is that counsellors create more problems than they cure, or even make people worse. Again, the myth is based on a grain of truth along with scanty understanding of the counselling process. If the counselling 'takes', because it is painful and involves change, signs of disturbances which were previously defended against do show. It is not that problems have been created, but that they have been brought to the surface instead of being left buried to have an insidious effect on the individual's functioning. A counsellor on the premises does implicitly sanction the acknowledgement of problems, and those in difficulty will come forward, making it appear that the counsellor has created the problems. The fault lies not in the counsellor, but in primitive logic.

VALUE CONFLICTS

These and no doubt other phantasies and myths perpetuate the idea that what counsellors do is outside the main purpose of the organization, and this seems confirmed when differing value systems and priorities clash over a particular individual. Someone who isn't working well may be exhorted by those responsible for his performance to pull up his socks, stay out of the pub, get himself organized. For those who need to be bullied or to feel guilty in order to work such an approach works, and success justifies the assumption that he could if he only would. A counsellor, however, may feel that this is a short-term, emergency solution which consigns the individual to a lifetime of threats and coercion with no enjoyment and satisfaction in work; and she may want to explore why that person needs to rest on such negative relationships. This is not likely to result in an immediate spurt of work, and the 'lazy' person may go through even more disruptive phases of depression and anxiety before his work goes smoothly. The conflict of values between one whose professional reputation relies on well-functioning, integrated individuals and another whose reputation depends on good work efficiently produced is obvious, and the client in the middle is in a marvellous position to play off the two against each other.

Richard seldom attended lectures and did very little work. His essays showed signs of a lively and clever mind, but they were incoherent, factually incorrect and often bizarre. His tutor, knowing he had a 'history', but not knowing the details, vacillated between sympathy and exasperation, and eventually sought guidance from the counsellor about how to manage Richard. One day he brought Richard in personally with all the signs of a worn-out and harassed parent, and the three talked. Richard told them that his father had put tremendous emphasis on academic success, even leaving the family behind when his job required him to move so Richard could do 'A' levels at his familiar school. While away, father died mysteriously - suicide and murder were both suspected - but the family never really accepted his death. Richard sometimes felt very sorry for himself, sometimes went out to look for father, and sometimes felt very guilty about his obvious impending failure. In the interview, the tutor took an increasingly stern line as Richard attacked him by cynically denigrating his subject with specious arguments. The counsellor grew increasingly concerned as Richard's confusion and anger and feeling that his father's death was a high cost to pay for a good education came out. The potential split was prevented because all three could together see how Richard drove his tutor into anger and retaliation, and how he was himself needing to mourn his father instead of attacking all the authorities around him. Weeks of counselling didn't enable him to pass his exams, but the hopeful signs meant he was given another chance.

Basic differences in priorities are realistically difficult to accommodate, but they can be if both parties are willing to test out their phantasies and negotiate their priorities. Frequently they will find that they do share values and together they can find means to an end that is wholly in their, the client's, and the organization's best interests. A counsellor in a college, for instance, if she is sufficiently identified with it and its aims, undoubtedly values education and has experienced the rewards of studying and good results, even though she may recognize that, for some students, academic work is temporarily or permanently inappropriate and beyond their intellectual or emotional capabilities. She will also be aware of the difficulties (personal and professional) faced by the teaching staff when a student fails or is disruptive, and she can take those into account. Conversely, staff who consult with or refer to a counsellor have some sympathy with her aims and some need for her particular expertise.

Miss T. was frequently consulted by a head of department in the college about failing students, but most of his staff avoided her. When Oliver failed dramatically in one subject, however, his tutor reluctantly (and more or less under order from the head) rang Miss T., asking for her opinion about the student since he wished to argue for an exception to the regulations so this 'blot' wouldn't show on an otherwise good record. He thought that Oliver had simply been lazy (he had said 'don't ask me to be ambitious because I'm not') but realized that that explanation would be harmful. Miss T. agreed to see Oliver, but made two crucial points to the tutor first: it was not her job to make the decision about suspending regulations, and she could only attempt to find out why Oliver had failed; and secondly, laziness was seldom simple laziness – there usually is some reason for a student's failure to work. The tutor was sceptical and hinted that he didn't really expect any help from her anyway.

Oliver came very late for his appointment, but they were none the less able to come to some understanding of his situation. He had failed that subject because it was genuinely difficult for him and he had lost interest in it. He was, by his own account, bright and naturally gifted and so had always managed to do well without trying. Once he had to try, like practising tennis or really tackling a subject, he lost interest and started something new. With a sustained degree course, however, he couldn't switch around like that and indeed his academic standard had steadily declined as the material became more difficult and sophisticated. It seemed to Miss T. that his future was jeopardized by this rather passive and omnipotent attitude to work. He agreed that he was in real trouble if he didn't change his approach, and accepted the idea of having counselling to sort himself out.

This was discussed with the tutor, with the boy's permission, who was dissatisfied because it was so psychological and hard to reshape into a respectable academic argument. As they discussed his problem of transforming the evidence in terms of the regulations, the tutor revealed that he had been aware of Oliver's steady decline and presumed he had been remiss in not dealing with it earlier, but he had assumed this promising student would, in the end, sail through the course. Miss T. responded in circumspectly general terms about the guilt and disappointment aroused by failing students, and raised the question of who was responsible for whether or not students used the opportunities given to them for learning. Almost despite himself, the tutor warmed to these issues, talked about his views and dilemmas, and having talked it through, could see his way to making an effective argument on behalf of the student, including Miss T's point that Oliver should understand that, with tuition and counselling offered, should he fail again, it was entirely his responsibility; it was not incumbent on the department to make further exceptions for him.

In this case, by the end of the transaction, each had done his job and only his job, responsibility was placed where it belonged, and initial antagonism between counsellor and tutor changed into a constructive working relationship which looked after both the individual's and the department's interests. Without doubt this happened because both were capable of identifying simultaneously with the individual and the organization and could explore the personal and professional matters from the security of clearly stated role and task boundaries.

It does frequently happen that consultations about a client are not just that, and the counsellor may more usefully respond to hints that the consulter wants a chance to discuss his dilemmas about decisions and policies. In fact, many management decisions can be made entirely without reference to the details of the client raising the problem, with the counsellor negotiating an advisory role. Such hints will only be heard if the counsellor has an impartial stance and can maintain a perspective (much as with individual clients) which encompasses the total situation, and neither enters into a conspiratorial *folie à deux* with the client to outwit the organization so he gets what he wants, nor sells out to the organization and is used to make its unpopular decisions. The temptations are strong, because, on the one hand, she wants to defend and protect the 'poor client', while, on the other, she needs to remain acceptable to the 'establishment' which probably pays her salary. A mediating or advisory role also exposes her diagnostic and prognostic skills and, in so far as these are used as evidence in a decision, she shares responsibility for that decision and its consequences. Finally, consultations involving a client usually arouse a counsellor's anxiety about confidentiality, and this may result in awkward and divisive incidents.

CONFIDENTIALITY AND COLLABORATION

Confidentiality is a vexed but rather overplayed issue in counselling. It is quite rightly at the centre of ethical and practical considerations because the client needs to feel safe from indiscriminate exposure and betrayal if he is to talk about himself at all honestly; but this protection seems to solidify imperceptibly into a defence designed to repel invaders. In an exchange between one who has and another who wants information about a client, there is ample room for jealous and tantalizing manoeuvres and the significant changes which occur when the counselling pair has to expand to include a third person do allow for distortion and abuse, not least because what was originally offered by the client as part of his self-exploration may now have to serve a purpose involving judgements. But a counsellor's suspicious anxiety about the three-way communication will surely be met by hostility and groundless speculation in the other, and that merely increases the likelihood of bad feelings between colleagues and of jeopardy to the client's well-being.

Part of the difficulty seems to lie in the ever-present possibility that the counselling room will convert itself into a confessional or a *boudoir* with deleterious consequences for the meaning of the transaction between counsellor and client. Some clients overtly regard counselling as a kind of confession, and they bring their foibles and upsets, hoping to have them magically absolved or obliterated. They correspondingly invite the counsellor to be omnipotent and to observe the sanctity of the confessional, sealing her lips at any enquiry – an invitation easily enough accepted, especially when the content is troublesome to the conscience of either. The *boudoir*, in contrast, is about excitement: the two are closeted together sharing intimacies, both gratified to be included and to have the power to exclude others. Both the *boudoir* and the confessional occur in a vacuum and ignore the wider reality of the client's life. Sins and secrets, absolution and excitement, are not the business of counselling. Confidences may be conveyed in the sense that the client imparts deeply private thoughts and feelings, but this is the medium, not the purpose, of the work which aims to integrate the client's internal and external reality. Because the client and the counselling exist in a context, sometimes the work will necessarily and profitably involve active collaboration with others in that environment.

There are no hard and fast rules about confidentiality – except perhaps that it is always a mistake to respond to a request with a tight-lipped and final 'I have nothing to say' – but, as the two-person relationship becomes a three-cornered interaction and the value and meaning of the communications change accordingly, the answers to some questions will provide guidelines for deciding whether it is in the client's interest to share or withhold information.

The first question is whether the counsellor has anything relevant to say. In the instance of a very specific request, she may have nothing to contribute, either because she simply doesn't know, or because the kind of information she holds is not appropriate to the request.

A government agency had a difficult legal decision to make about an individual and contacted her counsellor, who correctly insisted that his knowledge of her was not pertinent to the legal problem. Under pressure, however, he yielded and supplied some general information about her circumstances, with the result that the official was confused and compromised by now having knowledge which he didn't want and didn't know what to do with. On that occasion both parties paid for their indiscretion with considerable anxiety.

When, however, the counsellor does have something germane to say, she needs to choose what, among everything, is adequate to the context of the request and how best to express it. If an employer consults a counsellor about an employee's work problem, he wants to know only how the client's personal difficulties relate to that problem, and he needs the information in language applicable to his problem of management. Here, as we have already seen, the counsellor has to discover the nature of the management decision before she can decide what to say.

The second question, then, is how her information might be used not only organizationally, but also by the specific individual requesting it. This entails finding out whether that person is entitled, by role or relationship, to information, and how his emotional relationship with the client might colour the meaning or use of certain pieces of information. A client's depression over a broken love affair, for instance, could variously arouse sympathy, anger, impatience or triumph in others. An employer may have a right to know that the client is legitimately depressed, but the cause of that depression obviously needs to be kept from anyone who could use it, either interpersonally or managerially, to the client's detriment. It is also worth remembering here that sensitivity and shame are highly subjective: what is shameful or uncomfortable to one may not be to another; and, depending on the relationship, what a client would happily reveal to one person he might want to hide from someone else. A counsellor will clearly avoid conveying any information which will result in further discomfort or trouble for the client, both practically and emotionally, and to that end she needs to sift all she hears about the overt and covert reasons for collaboration for signs of manipulation and ulterior motives.

Along with questions about the context of the problem and people involved, the counsellor needs to consider how she might be being exploited in the three-way relationship. It's not uncommon for counsellors to be implicitly asked to take on someone else's responsibility or battle.

Stephen had been sent for counselling by his parents because they were unhappy about his refusal to continue his education or get a job. Although worried about himself, he was a reluctant client, resenting parental pressure to do something constructive. His father worked for an international organization, so they had moved frequently. Stephen felt the contradiction of being told to settle down when his family never had, and his feelings about this were discussed. Before his next appointment an irate letter from Father arrived, stating that his son had reported that it was all his (Father's) fault and criticizing the counsellor for her incompentence and impertinence in blaming him when he had done everything possible for the boy. The distortions contained in the letter suggested that the central issues were the current family strife and all their feelings about moving, and only work with the entire family would be fruitful. But Stephen, having started a fight between Father and counsellor, had decided to go on holiday, so only the parents could be seen. In the face of hostile questions about Stephen and what had transpired in the interview with him, the counsellor steadfastly explained that she was now responding to the letter and the family situation and wasn't prepared to answer their questions because that would only fuel a family fight. By discussing how she was being used to take Stephen's part and by pointing to their shared experience of Stephen opting out again rather than facing his conflict between wishing to support and to attack his parents, the parents could explore their part in the fight and their aspirations for the family, including the father's guilt in having to decide between geographical stability for the family and his career and financial ambitions. Clearly they appreciated Stephen's confusion, but he made them feel so guilty that they could only respond with anger. In this session the counsellor actually had to reveal nothing of the first interview, although her experience with Stephen helped her to understand the family problems.

This example shows that sometimes it is essential to work with others to provide a system of support for the client and to achieve some clarity in that system, even when the risk of breaking confidentiality is high. Within both organizations and families when a young person is struggling with internal conflicts and is testing the limits, joint efforts on the part of those around him are reassuring and containing and reduce his chances of wasting time and energy on unproductive fights and splits.

On the whole it is legitimate to share only that information which has already been worked on with the client: only then can the counsellor be confident that she has disentangled reality and phantasy, and has made fair inferences from what she has heard. Furthermore, the client has the right to know first, and a thorough discussion between them is an essential preliminary to any colleague exchange. This will include an exploration of the whys and wherefores of the collaboration, during which the counsellor makes the limits of her role and responsibility clear to the client. She will also share with him the general themes and data she may have in mind to disclose, not only so he will be familiar with them and will know where he stands with the third person when they next meet, but also so he may confirm that what she intends is acceptable to him, both generally and in the matter of its detail. If it isn't acceptable then further work between them is required. Obviously it's not possible to rehearse and anticipate all contingencies, so this prior discussion serves the purpose of establishing trust between client and counsellor, giving the counsellor confidence and permission to use her own judgement within the agreed limits. Occasionally there is no opportunity for such full discussion beforehand. In these cases the counsellor has to rely solely on her evaluation of how much disclosure the client will tolerate, and it is incumbent on her to report back to the client and work with his reactions. If the therapeutic alliance is good, this seldom creates problems; indeed clients are seldom as sensitive about confidentiality as they are imagined to be, especially when they are confident, on the basis of experience so far, that the counsellor is trustworthy.

The counsellor's discretion and trustworthiness is a matter of concern to her colleagues as well. Through clients she will hear about them and how they are perceived to conduct themselves in the assumed privacy of the office or lecture-room, and they will quite naturally be anxious about what she has heard, how accurate it is, and how that information will fare in her possession. Professionals work principally alone, unseen by colleagues. The absence of scrutiny and judgement is a relief to most, but the accompanying absence of evaluation and feedback leaves some prone to profound uncertainty about their professional competence. The notion that the counsellor can scrutinize and evaluate on the basis of comments of dubious veracity (leaving aside the tarnished phantasy of the analyst's X-ray eyes) not surprisingly makes colleagues uneasy with her. Paradoxically, this very cause of prickliness is the one totally shared aspect of their work. She also works privately, unobserved and unevaluated, and she too has to bear the anxiety of knowing that clients will talk about her to others – sometimes accurately; sometimes under the influence of a negative transference; sometimes in the equally distorting glow of idealization. This can be discussed, but colleagues, like clients, will be most firmly assured that their reputations are safe with her when they see her being consistently discrete and discerning in her dealings with others.

When the circumstances for sharing are fully understood dynamically and are acceptable, collaboration usually benefits all concerned, but there are instances when a client's material absolutely needs to be confidential. This happens when highly exciting or disturbing topics are involved, and the counsellor is tempted to burst out with it elsewhere. With exciting information the problem is to avoid falling into the *boudoir* mentality; but with disturbing material the problem is containing anxiety. Clients will dump their distasteful material on the counsellor because they can't stand it and want to get rid of it. The effect is noticeable – they feel relieved but she feels uncomfortable and likewise wants to dump it on someone else. The risk is that no one will tackle the material and it will hover around as an unmodified, useless and persecuting presence. The client will get the message that the topic is too difficult and is best avoided, and the 'spillage' both weakens and diminishes the client because what belongs inside is now outside and stands only a poor chance of being integrated.

In the end, confidentiality is largely an institutional issue, and when it is subjected to the same discrimination as the communication processes within the counselling relationship itself, it provides an opportunity for mending rather than confirming the split between counsellors and others in an organization. Stigma and stereotypes are only gradually dissolved, but the more frequently a counsellor can demonstrate through her professional relationships that there is no inherent incompatibility between the welfare of an organization and the well-being of those who belong to it in whatever capacity, the more successfully the counselling function will be retrieved from the outpost, and can make an integral contribution to the organization. Relieved of the attributes of failure, madness, softness, secrecy, and magic, counsellors have much to offer to the daily activities of the workplace. They are seldom, if ever, employed as agents of change, but their considerable knowledge of people and the ordinary business of living and working is equally seldom requested, and that is the organization's loss. Her training and skills are, after all, as appropriate to (and perhaps more effectively used in) preventing problems and helping to make the already good even better as they are to mopping up after things have gone wrong.

8 || Postscript

Nearly all the clients mentioned in this book gained from counselling, some minimally, some substantially, some after a single meeting, some after years of work. But there are still some who went away bitter and disappointed after a tussle with their problems or their counsellor. In my training and supervisory roles, I have watched many counsellors at work and have been impressed that such a diverse bunch of people, each putting his or her individual stamp on the work, could be effective. But there are still some who apparently do all the 'right' things yet seldom make any headway with their clients. That made me wonder what it is that makes counselling work for this tremendous variety of people and partnerships. A collection of stock phrases readily spring to mind, and they probably sum up all 1 have written.

Counselling works because it helps to reduce confusion: a great deal of distress and disorder arise because we simply can't make sense of some incidents in our history, our over-reaction to apparently innocent events, our tendency to do precisely the opposite of what we intend. Counselling acquaints us with both our unconscious life and with our personal interpretation of the facts of our lives, thereby giving sense to the senseless, and removing the discomfort and anxiety which inevitably accompany confusion.

Counselling works because it turns the past into memories: we actively carry with us past, untended wounds, unsatisfied wishes, unresolved anxieties, and we look for someone or something in the present to put them right. But usually we ask that of the 'wrong' person or opportunity, so the problems are entrenched and perpetuated. In any case, the past cannot be wiped out, but feelings about it can change, anachronistic needs and wishes can be placed in their proper historical context and relationships, and we can give up futile hoping for what can never be because the time is past. Counselling frees us to have what is available in the present.

Counselling works because it mends splits: we have disowned or denied wishes, needs and feelings which have been troublesome (creating too much anxiety and guilt), but what we have gained in defensive comfort we have lost in personal richness. By rediscovering and making friends with those repudiated aspects of ourselves, we can sort out how much – if at all – we need realistically be anxious and guilty, and we can recover useful resources for living our lives more fully and with greater satisfaction.

Counselling works because it makes us our own masters: by learning about our split-off bits, anxieties and defences, and out-of-date strivings which contribute to unconscious drives, we gain the means to depose those invisible slave-drivers and annex their considerable energy to make decisions, to venture where we will instead of scurrying around to avoid nameless and imaginary perils, and to have the life we want within only realistic constraints.

Counselling works because it is a place for 'working through': this is a hallowed concept in the psychoanalytic world, because it seems to be the essential therapeutic ingredient of the relationship. Change is seldom dramatic and immediate: again and again the client brings his anxieties and unconscious strivings into the transference relationship and tests them out against the reality of the therapeutic alliance. Each time they change or lessen a little until they can be relinquished as unnecessary, fruitless or misguided. Then there will come that moment of delightful recognition that relationships and activities outside the counselling room are also less fraught and more gratifying.

All these processes may be going on apace, but perhaps counselling really only works when the client is willing to undergo the uncertainty of change and the counsellor is willing to stand beside him and share the grief and excitement. Unless they can engage emotionally and draw out each other's willingness to work, nothing will happen. Ultimately, I think, this means they both appreciate the value of pain and can allow sorrow and tribulation to make their contribution to happiness. Ted, after years of work which saw unutterable depression, violence, hospitalization, divorce and unemployment in its course, had this to say at the end: 'We've got where we headed for – we've arrived at the station. And it's been the pretty route. No? Well, you have to agree there have been interesting scenes along the way.'

Bibliography

Bion, W. (1961) *Experience in Groups*, London, Tavistock Publications.

Blos, P. (1962) *On Adolescence*, New York, Free Press.

Curle, A. (1972) *Mystics and Militants*, London, Tavistock Publications.

de Board, R. (1978) *The Psychoanalysis of Organizations*, London, Tavistock Publications.

de Saint-Exupéry, A. (1945) *The Little Prince*, London, William Heinemann.

Dolto, F. (1974) *Dominique: Analysis of an Adolescent*, London, Souvenir Press.

Ezriel, H. (1963) 'Experimentation within the psychoanalytic session' in Paul, L. (ed.) *Psychoanalytic Clinical Interpretation*, New York, Free Press, 112-42.

Freud, A. (1937) *The Ego and Mechanisms of Defence*, London, Hogarth Press.

Freud, S. (1960) 'The psychopathology of everyday life', *The Standard Edition of the Complete Psychological Works*, vol. 6, London, Hogarth Press.

Freud S. (1961) 'The Ego and the id', *The Standard Edition of the Complete Psychological Works*, vol. 19, London, Hogarth Press.

Guntrip, H. (1968) *Schizoid Phenomena, Object Relations and the Self*, London, Hogarth Press.

Guntrip, H. (1970) *Your Mind and Your Health*, London, George Allen & Unwin.

Hesse. H. (1961) *The Prodigy*, London, Peter Owen.

Illich, I. (1975) *Medical Nemesis: The Expropriation of Health*, London, Calder & Boyars.

Kahn, M. (1974) *The Privacy of the Self*, London, Hogarth Press.

Klein, M. (1959) 'Our adult world and its roots in infancy', *Human Relations* 12, 291-303.

Lomas, P. (1973) *True and False Experience*, Harmondsworth, Allen Lane.

Malan, D. (1979) *Individual Psychotherapy and the Science of Psychodynamics*, London, Butterworth & Co.

Marris, P. (1974) *Loss and Change*, London, Routledge & Kegan Paul.

Meeks, J. (1971) *The Fragile Alliance*, Baltimore, Williams & Wilkins.

Menzies, I. (1977) *The Functioning of Social Systems as a Defence against Anxiety*, London, Tavistock Institute of Human Relations.

Parkes, C. (1972) *Bereavement*, London, Tavistock Publications.

Pincus, L. (1976) *Death and the Family*, London, Faber & Faber.

Pincus, L. and Dare, C. (1978) *Secrets in the Family*, London, Faber & Faber.

Rycroft, C. (1968) *Anxiety and Neurosis*, Harmondsworth, Allen Lane.

Segal, H. (1979) *Klein*, London, Fontana.

Strachey, J. (1934) 'The nature of the therapeutic action of psycho-analysis', *International Journal of Psychoanalysis* 15; 127-59.

Winnicott, D. (1971) *Playing and Reality*, London, Tavistock Publications.

Winnicott, D. (1972) *The Maturational Process and the Facilitating Environment*, London, Hogarth Press.

Wolfe, T. (1947) *You Can't Go Home Again*, London, William Heinemann.

Index

CLIENT EXAMPLES